"Why Fly That Way?"

Linking Community and Academic Achievement

"Why Fly That Way?"

Linking Community and Academic Achievement

Kathy Greeley

Foreword by Deborah Meier

Teachers College
Columbia University
New York and London

Published by Teachers College Press, 1234 Amsterdam Avenue, New York, NY 10027

Library of Congress Cataloging-in-Publication Data

Greeley, Kathy.
  "Why fly that way?" : linking community and academic achievement / Kathy Greeley ; foreword by Deborah Meier.
    p. cm.
  Includes bibliographical references (p.) and index.
  ISBN 0-8077-3980-4 (pbk. : alk. paper)
    1. Social values—Study and teaching (Middle school)—United States.
  2. Community—Study and teaching (Middle school)—United States.
  3. Classroom environment—United States. 4. Academic achievement—United States. I. Title.
  LC192.4 .G74 2000
  306.43'2—dc21   00-041778

ISBN 0-8077-3980-4 (paper)

Printed on acid-free paper

Manufactured in the United States of America

07 06 05 04 03 02 01 00   8 7 6 5 4 3 2 1

For all the students of Room 311
who learned to fly in the V

and

For Megan, Zoë, and Dan

Contents

Foreword *by Deborah Meier*   ix

Acknowledgments   xi

Introduction   xiii

 1. **The End of the Year**   1
 2. **The Class From Hell**   8
 3. **The Parable of the Geese**   16
 4. **Expert Projects**   22
 5. **Sameness v. Difference**   39
 6. **Skating in the V**   47
 7. **Exclusion Acts**   53
 8. **Making Connections**   62
 9. **Taking the Leap**   67
10. **Warm-ups**   76
11. **Finding the Story**   82
12. **A Script Emerges**   88
13. **Adding Music**   98
14. **The Performance**   104
15. **Lessons Learned**   113

References   127

Index   129

About the Author   133

Foreword

"Why Fly That Way?" is a story told by a teacher who is not afraid to dream. She uses those dreams to reshape the here and now of classroom life. Her story starts with the woes, which I recognize all too well. It's full of the suspense, the drama of the school year as it unfolds.

Kathy Greeley argues that building a classroom community is critically important to raising academic achievement. Any time we practice our craft of teaching without first building bonds between learners, we do grave personal injury to many of our students and simultaneously fail to teach most of them well. In the absence of a safe environment, even learning something like the times tables can be subverted, much less the tougher or more rigorous academic tasks.

The way one goes about building the space for the intellectual risks that learning demands is an art that Kathy Greeley lays out before us. By showing us how it can be done for the early adolescents in her class, she helps us see how we might do it for all our students and ourselves in all our schools, in our workplaces, and even in our own families. In fact, she shows us what it would take for a serious democratic debate to take place in this country, by using the kind of intellectual tools we need to challenge each other in the way democracy requires. Thus, this is a book not only about the requirements of good schooling but also about the requirements for building good democracies. This is the hardest and toughest work a school can take on. It is, without question, what is necessary if we are to produce the kind of high-achieving schools that most Americans say we need, and which we are fast losing sight of in our mania for more and more anonymous and mindless test-focused schooling.

In most societies, the ages between 12 and 14 are the ritualized time for becoming an adult—and all eyes are focused on the child's transition to adulthood. Through most of human history, this age has signaled growing responsibility and an increasing connectedness to the adult world. In our lifetimes, however, it has become a period of uselessness and increasingly, estrangement, separateness, and isolation—the peak years for irresponsibility, not responsibility. At the same time, school has become larger and more anonymous, teachers more distant, parents and grandparents less accessible (and often working).

Fortunately, some educators see in teenagers the possibilities for the best of childhood and adulthood rather than the worst of both. They have ideas about what would be good for students this age, and for the larger society. While keeping expectations high and standards rigorous, they seek ways to make learning make sense, to find connection between young people's lives and curriculum goals. These educators have built an always fragile and threatened middle school movement. There are a growing number of such folk, and Kathy Greeley speaks eloquently for them and their ideas.

Real school life, as Kathy captures it on these pages, is full of stories: serious stories, funny stories, stories that need to be told with great love and affection. Sometimes it's hard to see how the affection can stay so strong. This book reads easily—I'd recommend reading it once for the sheer fun of watching a master class unfold before your eyes, and then again to see what it can teach you about the ways we all need to interact with our children. And maybe even with each other.

Deborah Meier

Acknowledgments

In 1995, I had the opportunity to take a year off from teaching and attend Harvard's Graduate School of Education. There I met Eleanor Duckworth who became both my academic advisor and my friend. One day in January I found myself sitting in her small, cluttered office wringing my hands about what to do in my second semester. There were so many interesting courses to take, so many interesting people with whom to study, so little time in which to do it all.

But, I told Eleanor, I couldn't shake this idea that had been stewing in my head for a while about writing something about the previous year in my classroom. After listening to me babble on for about 15 minutes, Eleanor said, "Kathy, it sounds like you really want to write this story. You can do it as an independent study with me. You should stop talking about it and just do it."

That was the official beginning of this project. Armed with Eleanor's vote of confidence, I cleared both my calendar and my desk with great excitement. I sat down at my computer only to experience a major moment of panic. What made me think this story was so important after all? I had no idea where to begin. I was drawing a total blank.

After a few hours of trying to plow through my serious writer's block, I called my friend and colleague Jackie Honig. Jackie had worked in the classroom with me throughout that year. "Don't panic," she said. "I'll help you get started." We began meeting once a week at the local coffeehouse. Every Friday for several months we would talk about students, activities, projects we had done, lessons we had learned together, all the ups and downs, highs and lows that had happened during that year. Jackie urged me to trust my voice. She read drafts, reminded me of things I had missed, shared her own notes, helped me to clarify my thoughts. Gradually the story began to emerge.

.

There are several other people who also played an important part in helping this book come together whom I would like to thank. Susan Liddicoat of Teachers College Press worked with me to turn the original manuscript, something more like a long article, into the book it is now. Jim Beane, after reading a couple of drafts, offered poignant critique and probing questions that helped me reflect on the lessons of the year. Leah Rugen and Susan Miller both read and reread early drafts and gave critical yet supportive feedback. At a later point, Susan McCray, "Doc" and Priscilla Howe, and Maryel Locke gave good editorial suggestions and a lot of encouragement to keep going.

I would also like to acknowledge some of the people who have had a profound influence on my classroom over the years. As I look back over this manuscript, I see the lessons learned from Ron Berger, an outstanding sixth-grade teacher in Shutesbury, Massachusetts, and Steve Seidel, at Harvard's Project Zero, in every page. Their commitment to quality and excellence for all children and their belief that *all* children are gifted continue to inspire me. In addition, Steve Seidel and Diana Moller introduced me and my students to the wonderful world of theater. They have played critical roles in guidance and support throughout every production I have ever done, whether they know it or not. It was Diana and Jackie who helped me to be comfortable in "the gray space." I am also very grateful to Judith Contrucci, John Bay, and the Cambridge Middle School Drama Collaborative for all their support to my classroom.

Finally, I have to thank my husband Dan and my daughters Zoë and Megan for their love, for believing in me and my mission, and for having the patience to put up with me during the difficult times, both as writer and teacher. Dan supported me at every stage of this process. He encouraged me to write, he edited and gave feedback on numerous drafts, he helped me with research, he urged me on when I got frustrated, and he inspired me with his own commitment to quality education for all children.

Introduction

Every teacher knows that each school year is different; each class has its own unique chemistry, rhythm, history. Each year of teaching carries its own successes and failures. And, it's to be hoped, each year the teacher also gains a little more insight into the mysterious art and difficult craft of teaching.

This is a story about just one classroom during one academic year. Why tell the story of this particular class during this particular year? I've asked myself that many times. Why have I felt so compelled to record *this* particular story? I have certainly had other classes that were much easier and more fun to teach than this group. In fact, this bunch arrived in my classroom with a rather wretched reputation, much of it deserved, I quickly discovered.

Perhaps this specific group stands out not because of what the students were or were not but because of what they *became*. There were many challenges, difficulties, obstacles, and failures. There were times of despair and frustration. At times I felt totally ineffectual and defeated. And yet, gradually, I saw a motley crew of insecure, resistant, fearful, and at times mean-spirited young adolescents become a community willing to work through difficulties together, tolerate and appreciate differences, take risks and go beyond their "comfort zone," and let themselves care. I realized, by the end of the year, that I had witnessed a real transformation—both of individuals and of the class as a whole. I felt an urgency to write down their story because I didn't want to forget how we got there.

What were the driving forces behind this transformation? Although many factors were involved, one of the most important was our ongoing commitment to building community in the classroom. I learned from these young people that when students feel safe, when they feel respect from both their peers and their teachers, and when they trust the people around them, they become free to learn. They are able to engage in the practices that lead to authentic intellectual growth. They become more willing to say what they think, more willing to share their work and invite feedback, more willing to experiment and try new things, more willing to try again when they don't get it right the first time, and more willing to invest in their own learning. And, because of this, they become better readers, writers, and thinkers.

Primary-grade teachers seem to understand this. We all remember *All I Really Need to Know I Learned in Kindergarten* (Fulghum, 1993). Primary teachers, at least good ones, are careful to teach children how to be respectful of themselves and others. They pay attention to children's feelings and understand that when children feel safe, respected, and appreciated, they learn better. But generally, as students move up grade levels, less attention is paid to the culture of the classroom. Less time is spent in developing that sense of community. Teachers say they don't have *time* to focus on "touchy-feely" stuff anymore. They have to focus on academics. They have too much information that must be imparted. Curriculum to cover. We are supposed to pour knowledge into students' heads. We are the givers, they are the receivers—or, even more passively, the vessels. Some teachers make token attempts to create a sense of community and respect because, after all, everyone would rather teach a class that has it than one that doesn't. But most teachers don't see it as essential to the learning process and therefore don't continue to make the time for it.

But I argue that when we create a strong sense of community in our classrooms, we *enhance* academic learning. This point was made dramatically in the film *Eye of the Storm* based on the well-known "blue eyes, brown eyes" experiment. In this third-grade classroom simulation on discrimination, students with blue eyes were asked to wear flannel collars for a day, denoting them as an "inferior" group. When they sat down with their teacher to do a flash-card exercise, their performance times fell dramatically from those of the day before. When the teacher asked them what was wrong, why they hadn't been able to do nearly as well with the cards as they had just the day before, the children replied that it was the collars' fault. They said they were distracted and couldn't concentrate. After experiencing exclusion, discrimination, and ridicule from peers (behaviors that can be common to the middle school experience), their previously safe community had been destroyed for that day. Interestingly, when the collars were removed, the children's scores improved dramatically and in fact exceeded their scores of previous days. What accounted for this? They had not received remedial math help. Rather, the sense of equality, respect, and community had been restored to the classroom. I believe students will achieve more when we create a climate in which they feel safe and are willing to take risks.

In addition to academic benefits, there is another important reason schools need to pay attention to classroom culture and community building. Although the goal of public schooling has been fiercely debated over the years, most people would agree that preparing students to be productive members of both their local communities and the larger democracy is essential. Alexis de Tocqueville said that education in a democracy must be "an apprenticeship in liberty." In the early 1900s, John Dewey wrote that a democratic society "must have a type of education which gives individuals a personal interest in social relationships and control, and the habits of mind which secure social changes without introducing disorder" (quoted in Noddings, 1999, p. 580). Carl Glickman (1993), writing some 150 years after de Tocqueville and several decades after Dewey, asserts,

> Public education is the only institution designated and funded as the agent of the larger society in protecting the core value of its citizens: democracy. . . . What difference does it make if we graduate 100 percent of our students, or if SAT scores rise twenty points, or if our students beat other countries in achievement in science when they have not learned how to identify, analyze, and solve the problems that face their immediate and larger communities? (pp. 8–9)

What we teach and how we teach it—both directly, in terms of our academic curriculum, and indirectly, in terms of the social curriculum we model—should reinforce our social ideals and values. However, far from becoming the "kinder and gentler nation" promised us years ago, our society seems increasingly anchorless and devoid of simple civility, assumptions of kindness, or even a fundamental respect for each other. Although the task of reclaiming our communities is far larger than schools can accomplish on their own, we can have an impact. The culture of the whole school—in the classroom, in the hallway, on the playground, in the cafeteria, on the bus—should reflect and reinforce what we strive for: respect, tolerance, hard work, informed literacy, and critical thinking.

In 1983, a National Commission on Excellence in Education proclaimed that our nation was at risk in a report that announced the failure of our schools to educate our children. It declared schools were soft on kids. It called for rigorous standards and a return to basics. It demanded that our youth be prepared to compete, and succeed, in the global marketplace.

A Nation at Risk launched debates concerning public education that continue to rage about curriculum, discipline, testing, and national standards. But there is a fundamental question that educators, parents, politicians, and community members should be asking first. What are we educating children for? How do we want them to use their education? What kind of people do we want them to be?

Several years ago, as I was preparing to teach a unit on the Holocaust, I came across a letter that a high school principal had written to his faculty (Strom & Parsons, 1982). His letter read:

> Dear Teacher:
>
> I am a survivor of a concentration camp. My eyes saw what no man should witness:
>
> Gas chambers built by learned engineers.
>
> Children poisoned by educated physicians.
>
> Infants killed by trained nurses.
>
> Women and babies shot and burned by high school and college graduates.
>
> So I am suspicious of education.
>
> My request is: Help your students become human. Your efforts must never produce learned monsters, skilled psychopaths, educated Eichmanns.
>
> Reading, writing, arithmetic are important only if they serve to make our children more human. (p. 166)

Nazi Germany provides but one example (albeit a powerful one) of how dangerously perverted education devoid of social values and critical thinking can be. One hundred and fifty years ago, Ralph Waldo Emerson gave a lecture at Harvard University in which he worried that

> institutions originally founded to teach their students how to become good and decent, as well as broadly and deeply literate, may abandon the first mission to concentrate on a driven, narrow book learning—a course of study in no way intent on making a connection between ideas and theories on one hand and, on the other, our lives as we actually live them. (as cited in Coles, 1995, p. A68)

Have schools forsaken "the first mission" to teach our students "how to become good and decent" to instead "concentrate on a driven, narrow book learning" in the present panicked pursuit of so-called academic rigor? Do these two missions of educating the heart and the mind have to be in conflict with each other? Do we have to choose between an educated person and a moral one? I don't think so. Children must learn about the world, but they must also learn how to be in the world. We can and must teach both academics and something much bigger, how to be human. In fact, I believe each type of learning can actually enhance the other. When we pay attention to the culture of community in our classrooms, we are not taking time *from* academics; we are building a foundation and a purpose *for* academics.

Emerson, in addition to reminding us of the broader goals of education, pointed out that education must connect ideas and theories with real life. We learn best when knowledge or information has immediate importance and authentic purpose or, as Deborah Meier (1995) says, "when our natural drive to make sense of things is allowed to flourish" (p. 152). Rather than supporting the opinion of those who insist our children need to learn endless lists of topics and facts, I believe that a rich, deep curriculum that taps into critical issues in young people's lives will motivate students to become not just memorizers but lifelong learners.

James Beane (1997) speaks of a holistic kind of curriculum integration (and reminds us of its deep historical roots), one that engages with the past, connects to the community, crosses subject boundaries, and connects meaningfully with students' lives. "With its emphasis on participatory planning, contextual knowledge, real-life issues, and unified organization, curriculum integration provides broad access to knowledge for diverse young people and thus opens the way for more success for more of them" (p. xi).

Ah, but can you prove it? Is there hard-core research connecting strong community, engaging and meaningful curriculum, and academic excellence? Where are your data? Do test scores go up? Is there a direct correlation between compassion and good spelling? Can you test for "kindness," "generosity," "good community member"? I do not have data and statistics to prove my point, but there is evidence.

The Child Development Project, based in Oakland, California, has studied several elementary and middle schools around the country. This project found:

At schools high in "community"—measured by the degree of students' agreement with statements such as "My school is like a family" and "Students really care about each other"—students show a host of positive outcomes. These include higher educational expectations and academic performance, stronger motivation to learn, greater liking for school, less absenteeism, greater social competence, fewer conduct problems, reduced drug use and delinquency, and greater commitment to democratic values. (Lewis, Schaps, & Watson, 1996, p. 17)

In *Literacies Lost*, M. Cyrene Wells (1996) describes a middle school in which the building of a democratic community, including students, teachers, administrators, and townspeople, was at the core of creating a school of excellence. We meet a group of students who feel real ownership over their own learning, who deeply pursue literacy in its broadest sense, who exhibit few disciplinary problems, and who feel responsible toward each other, their school, and their town. When graduates from this vibrant middle school went on to a traditional high school, students' enthusiasm for learning and working hard was quickly stamped out. As one student said, "I have so much to learn and I'm stuck here in this class" (p. 133).

There are other kinds of evidence, too. I first met Ron Berger, an extraordinary sixth-grade teacher, at a Harvard University institute on assessment. As people were milling about, waiting for the plenary session to begin, I noticed some beautiful architectural drawings displayed on the walls of the conference hall. Oh, I thought to myself, the Design School must have had a previous conference here.

I was soon to discover that the drawings had been done by Ron's sixth-grade class. These were not, he was careful to point out, so-called gifted and talented children. They were just his kids. When Ron's students were continually winning top prizes in state essay and poster contests, the Massachusetts Department of Education investigated their small rural school in Shutesbury. The department was suspicious of such success (much like Jaime Escalante's story in Los Angeles). How could these students do such outstanding work? Were they cheating somehow? What they found was a classroom, indeed a whole school, where students and teachers were committed to the highest standards of work, where students worked cooperatively to reach that goal, where students cared about what they were learning, where students learned to value each other for a range of talents and skills, both academic and other.

Ron explains the underlying philosophy that is the foundation of the school's success:

> The quality of a school lies in its culture. . . . The only way to understand a school culture is to understand what students experience in being part of it. Not just the motivated, mainstream students, but also the students who look or feel different. How safe do students feel, physically and emotionally? What kind of pride and intensity is encouraged for work? What values, what sense of courtesy and responsibility are modeled? A school culture of quality connotes a culture of high standards for *all* students in *all* domains: standards for academic achievement, arts, physical fitness, critical thinking, and creativity, but also standards for kindness, integrity, industriousness, and responsibility. (Berger, 1997, p. 11)

Luckily, Ron Berger is not the only teacher who is committed to creating this kind of culture in school. There are many more out there. In the current climate of testing mania, overly rigid curriculum frameworks, and a push for standardization rather than real standards, these voices need to be heard. The following story is about the class that convinced me of the critical importance of building a classroom community that nurtures basic democratic values like respect, tolerance, and compassion; developing rich, meaningful curriculum; and holding students to high academic standards.

"Why Fly That Way?"

Linking Community and
Academic Achievement

CHAPTER 1

The End of the Year

IT WAS THE LAST day of school. The eighth graders had graduated 2 weeks earlier. My seventh-grade homeroom and I were sitting in a circle on the rug in the back of the classroom and we were crying. It was very hard saying goodbye. It had been a remarkable year.

"I don't want this year to end," said Nierika.

"It won't be the same next year," said Leana.

"Why not?" I asked. "Why can't it be?"

"We know those sixth graders . . . I mean, the new seventh graders. They're different from us. We've never gotten along with them."

"We had such a community here," said Adam.

"What do you mean?" I pushed him.

"I mean, people felt safe with each other. People trusted each other. It won't be like that next year." Heads around the circle nodded.

"Why not?" I persisted. "We didn't start the year like this. We built it over time, by sharing our stories, by doing the play, through all the work we did together. You can build that feeling of community again when you're in Arthur's class."

"It just won't work with those kids," they all agreed.

Why not, I wondered.

I teach seventh- and eighth-grade humanities at the Graham and Parks School in Cambridge, Massachusetts. Located in a racially and economically diverse neighborhood, Graham and Parks, a K–8 school, has approximately 400 students. Of these, 54% are of color and 46% are White. Nearly a third of the students are Haitian because the city's primary Haitian bilingual program is housed here. Thirty-eight percent of the students qualify for free or reduced lunch, and nearly 40% have "special needs."

Cambridge has a controlled choice system inspired by its voluntary racial desegregation plan of the 1970s. Parents rank their choice of schools for their children, and most people receive one of their top three requests. Graham and Parks has consistently been one of the most requested schools in the city. Standardized test scores tend to be quite high, there is low staff turnover, parents are involved in decision-making at many levels, and the teachers have a reputation for dedication and innovative curriculum.

The first alternative, "open-education" program in the city, the school encourages active, hands-on, project-based learning. Many teachers use an integrated, thematic approach to curriculum. If you walk through the halls, you will see Egyptian sarcophagi attached to the walls, models of 19th-century Irish villages in display cases, a brilliantly colored mural with images from Haiti, annals of the Holocaust and the civil rights movement of the 1960s mounted on a stairwell, student-made flags representing the children's ethnic origins hanging from the ceiling of the first-floor corridor, as well as ever-changing displays of student work. If you enter a classroom, you might find yourself suddenly in a tropical rain forest, a Japanese village, or Salem, Massachusetts, witnessing the witchcraft trials.

Classes are multigraded and self-contained through the sixth grade. Class size averages 23 students per teacher. In the seventh and eighth grades, classes are semidepartmentalized and a little smaller. Students take math and science in grade-level groupings (because of the citywide mandate for eighth-grade algebra) but have the same math and science teachers for a 2-year curriculum cycle. Humanities classes, an integration of language arts and social studies, have a mixture of seventh- and eighth-grade students. There are four sections of humanities, each with 18 to 20 students, and two humanities teachers. Unlike in science and math, in humanities students have one teacher for one year and then switch to the other teacher's class for their second year.

Even though humanities classes are double-blocked for 100-minute periods, a lot must be covered in that time. We focus on building reading, writing, listening, and speaking skills while also including social studies skills and content. Each day begins with a "Daily Edit" to teach and review grammar and writing mechanics. We have small "Book Talk Groups" that meet regularly to discuss class novels. Vocabulary words come from the novels we are reading, class discussions, and the history we are studying. We work on both expository and creative writing. We try to interject as many current events as we can.

A few years ago when the middle school team decided to try the integrated humanities approach, inspired by the principles of the Coalition of Essential Schools, I began to structure my curriculum around a theme and some "essential" questions that could tie together the various threads of our academic study. A good "essential" question is one that does not have a clear, straightforward answer but rather is open-ended and provocative. A good "essential" question invites complexity and critical thinking. At the same time it requires students to gain knowledge and information, it pushes them to draw their own conclusions and encourages further questions.

I also felt that approaching the curriculum with a broad, overarching theme would help students to make connections between events in history, current issues, and their lives today. I wanted them to see how the study of history and literature was linked through universal themes that human beings have wrestled with across times and cultures. By exploring some of these questions, we could come to better understand our own humanity.

I looked for themes that would stimulate deep questions and allow us to make these kinds of connections. One year we focused on the American Dream. What makes America America? What is the American Dream? Do all people have access to it? Is there liberty and justice for all? During the year with Adam, Nierika, and Leana, we began by looking at the concept of *change*: How do societies change? How do individuals make change in their society? How are we, as individuals, changing? We grounded our examination of these questions in history and literature.

We started with an in-depth study of the Holocaust, using the *Facing History and Ourselves* curriculum (Strom & Parsons, 1982). This curriculum challenges students to reflect on the causes and consequences of intolerance, racism, violence, and passivity. It helps students to gain an in-depth understanding of the social, political, and economic factors that led to the rise of the Nazi Party in Germany in 1933 and the resulting Holocaust.

We took a similar approach to studying the Civil Rights Movement in the United States, examining the roots of the movement beginning with Reconstruction and tracing the path of the struggle for equality that eventually erupted in the 1950s and 1960s. We looked at how ordinary people were able to change history. As we explored both of these histories, we became intrigued with the idea of courage. What exactly is courage? Whom do we consider courageous and why? What makes ordinary people do extraordinary things? Can someone be both courageous and cowardly? How would I act if I were faced with similar choices?

Toward the end of that year, students wrote and produced a powerful play that gave voice to their own understanding of these issues. Over the years, producing a play had become both a hallmark of Room 311 and a key component of my curriculum. Our first play, *On the Line*, had been about the famous Bread-and-Roses Strike of 1912 in Lawrence, Massachusetts (Korty, 1979). Although the story focused on the life of a 14-year-old mill worker and the dilemmas she faced as her fellow workers walked off their jobs to protest for the 8-hour day, the play brought together themes we had been studying all semester: immigration, the industrial revolution, and the growth of the labor movement.

Through *On the Line*, I discovered the value of using theater in the classroom. As students "tried on" the lives of the characters in the play, they had an opportunity to explore historical content in a deep and rich way. They understood the personal courage it took to stand up for one's rights; they understood the cost to a whole family of losing one wage earner. But far from simply making history come alive, the process of making theater made students come alive too.

On the Line was written by a local playwright. When I decided to venture into the realm of original scripts and student-written plays, I made new discoveries about the power of theater in student learning. Through the process of creating a play that addressed the themes of our Holocaust and civil rights study, students were able to make their own meaning from the lessons of history. As they developed characters and a plot that avoided the simplistic style of TV Afternoon Specials, they had to confront the complexities of history both critically and creatively. Furthermore, through the process of creating and producing their own drama, students were able to put the lessons they had learned from history into practice. They not only learned about people who had worked together for a better world (the resisters and rescuers of the Holocaust and the activists of the Civil Rights Movement), but they also experienced a little of the power of this kind of collaboration themselves as they worked and reworked scripts. Students learned about people who had taken risks in the past, and, through drama, they too learned to take risks in experimentation and public performance. They read about people who had asked questions, challenged the status quo, and looked critically at personal choices, and, in order to create a quality piece of art, they looked deeply into themselves.

Another powerful element of playmaking I discovered that year was the kind of classroom culture it produced. I saw students give each other support, positive feedback, honest critique, and encouragement. They developed a deep trust in each other. As we crafted our art, a strong community emerged. In turn, this feeling of community fostered a willingness among students to care about the quality of their work, to dig deeply into historical material, and to push their own personal boundaries into new and unfamiliar territory. Adam, Nierika, and Leana were right. We had indeed created something very special in Room 311.

That summer, I thought a lot about that sense of community and the powerful learning it seemed to have inspired. Was it that particular group of students? Did they just have the right chemistry? They were a great bunch of kids, willing to try new things and work hard. Or was it the curriculum? We had dealt with powerful themes and delved deep into issues that touched students' lives. Or was it the unique configuration of adults? Winston, my aide, and Jackie and Sherri, two student teachers working with me, were deeply committed to young people. They brought talent, caring, and a willingness to go above and beyond the call of duty. Was it the play? Our standards were high and young people seemed to welcome the challenge. For the fourth year in a row, students had produced a piece of theater that captured real concerns and issues that young adolescents struggle with every day. Was I responsible? Was I finally, after 10 years, getting the knack of teaching?

Around the middle of August, we had some friends over for dinner. Steve and Adria were longtime friends, and their two sons had been students in my class. It was Adam who had been quite vocal on that last day of school about his fears for the upcoming year. Adam had just come back from a month away at camp and was full of enthusiasm.

"Camp was great," he said. "It was such an incredible community." That word again. My ears perked up, my teacher self kicked in.

"Why? How was it different from school? How did it feel different?"

"People were nice to each other. Everyone was relaxed. You could be yourself. People assumed that everyone would be nice, so you didn't have to be on guard. At school, you are always on guard."

I pressed Adam to describe how the camp created such a different environment.

"Well . . . circumstances are so different. School could never be like camp. After school you can go home and see other friends. But at camp you can't do that. You go back to your cabin and you are forced to be with kids whether you like them or not . . . but by the end of camp everyone feels real close. I've never had a cabin that I was really excited about at first . . . but by the end I always really liked the kids."

"So the main thing is you can't escape?"

"Yeah. But it is also . . . well, you know how we felt like more of a community after the play? We had created this thing that was really amazing. It's like that at camp; you have to work things out. You are facing problems that have to be answered and you have to figure out a way to do it. It's sort of inescapable . . . you know, you can't leave . . . like the play won't be any good if you don't figure out the answer . . . that helps people get closer and they help each other."

"How else is it different?"

"Well, at camp, the older kids don't lord it over younger kids. They sort of accept the idea of the community, they've been coming to the camp quite awhile so they know what their role as an older person has to be. They had looked up to the older kids when they were younger and they saw how they helped the community. So they assume that position."

"Why can't eighth graders set an example like that?" I asked. "You know, I've heard kids say they can't wait to be eighth graders so they can beat up on younger kids. Why would you want to do that when you know how crappy it felt?"

Adam laughed. "That's exactly why you want to do it—because you know how crappy it felt. They say, 'Hey, when I was a sixth grader I had to get beat up. Now it's your turn to get beat up and it's my turn to do it.'"

"Do you think it has to be that way?"

"I don't know," he shrugged. "But that's the way it is."

As I reflected on the previous year and on my conversation with Adam, the theme for the coming year became clear. We needed to explore this idea of *community*: What makes communities work? What breaks communities apart? What kind of community do we want? How do we work together as a community? Of course, other questions would also emerge from the students and from our work together.

To be effective, the theme had to be embedded in the content of the curriculum. In the coming school year, we planned to study 19th-century American history with a focus on immigration, slavery, the industrial revolution, and the growth of cities. What does community have to do with all that? We would discover powerful connections.

CHAPTER 2

The Class From Hell

EVERY TEACHER HAS HAD, at one time or another, "the class from hell." Sometimes we wonder if a problem arose with the water that year, or if the planets were crossed, or if some strange cosmic disturbance occurred that no one noticed at the time. The lessons that have always been successful with all your other classes just don't work with these kids. You go home wondering why you ever became a teacher. You think it might be time for a career change.

I had heard about these incoming seventh graders for years from other teachers in the school, and even from the eighth graders. But I ignored the horror stories. I make it a policy to ignore horror stories. Kids change. Teachers change. Dynamics change. Kids respond differently to different teachers. There are many factors that contribute to class chemistry. Furthermore, this year I had two wonderful young women working with me. Jackie Honig had worked with me the year before, and she was coming back to volunteer part-time. She already knew the ropes at Graham and Parks, and the kids loved her. June Parks, who worked as a part-time teaching aide, was a native Cantabridgian. She had grown up down the street from me, attended Cambridge Rindge and Latin School, and was interested in possibly pursuing a teaching career. With a team like this, I thought, we can take on anything.

On the first day of school, kids are nearly always on their best behavior. Many students want to get a good start to the year. They want to put their best foot forward and have high expectations for themselves. Others are tentative, nervous about what will be expected of them by these new teachers. Some are in a daze, still hung over from the intoxication of summer's freedom. It is the one day I can always count on feeling strong and in charge. After a few weeks, or with some classes after a few days, the honeymoon ends. Kids test the limits, boundaries are fought for and won, and by October the culture of the classroom has been established.

But this year was different. I don't remember exactly how the day went, but I knew from the moment the kids first burst through the door that it was going to be a challenging year.[1] They were difficult to quiet down. They ruthlessly interrupted each other. The eyerolling quotient was high. They seemed to be lacking some basic internal control mechanisms. At the end of the day, June, Jackie, and I sat staring at each other, slightly shellshocked. My first journal entry from that year reads:

> Day One. I'm exhausted. We had a ten minute break to wolf down food. These kids are something else. I remember my homeroom last year; I could barely get them to talk or open their mouths at first. These guys, I couldn't shut them up. And I'm not so sure how nice they are to each other. It's gonna take a lot of work to shape this group into a group. It does take a while for the personality of the class to emerge—but . . . I feel nervous. All my ideas, and ideals run smack into reality. I don't get much of a sense of connection from some kids. . . . Day One. I think it's going to be a long year.

After the first day of school, I realized that our theme of community was going to be both challenging and crucial to consider. In years past, I tended to leap into the curriculum content right away. This year, I decided to try a different tack.

"This year, we are going to be exploring the idea of community— what makes a strong community, what breaks it apart. Jesse, would you stop that and turn around? What is a community, anyway?" I asked. They all began talking at once. I called for attention and then nodded toward a girl whose hand was raised.

"A community is a group of people who live or work together," said one girl.

"Yeah, people share a common space and sometimes a common purpose," shouted out another student.

---

1. Although I was teaching two different sections of humanities, for the purposes of this account, I have not differentiated them. Even though each section had a somewhat different personality, the issues we were struggling with were quite similar. The curriculum was the same with each group, and the two classes moved along in parallel fashion.

"Nicole, please don't shout out. You need to raise your hand. So . . . does a common space and a common purpose make us a community?" I asked.

"Yeah," students chorused.

"We are a community because we all come together to learn. We have a common purpose," offered another girl seriously.

"She is such a little . . . ," muttered the boy next to her. I glared at him for a second. He looked away. I saw two boys tugging over a pencil. They stopped when they saw me looking at them.

"Does that make us a community?" I asked.

"Yeah," they chorused glibly.

"We'll see," I said. "We're going to give you a test to see what kind of community you are."

"A test?"

I asked students to clear their desks out of the way, took out 19 blindfolds, and gave one to each student. In the center of the room, I placed a large rope that was tied in a circle. Students gathered around the outside of the rope. I told them to put on their blindfolds and then pick up the rope with both hands.

"Now, without peeking, see if you can form a perfect triangle," I directed. There was a lot of giggling as they started shuffling around, pushing against each other.

"Don't push me!"

"What are we doing?"

"I think we should—"

"*I* think we should—"

"No, I have an idea—"

"Okay, let's get organized here. There are 19 of us so—"

"Ow! You're stepping on my foot!"

"This is stupid."

"You're stupid."

"We need three groups of six, plus one—"

"Why are we doing this?"

"Stop pushing."

"So count off by sixes."

"Who made you boss?"

"Well, somebody has to—"

"I think we should—"

"Move over, stupid—"

"I think we got it."

"Wait, this isn't right . . . "

I watched, wondering if they were ever going to succeed in this simple task. June looked on in disbelief. Jackie chuckled to herself at their disorder. Slowly, though, an equilateral triangle began to emerge. "Are you ready yet?" I asked.

"NO!" they yelled back. They kept jostling, trying to check their shape.

"Let me know when you are ready," I said. After a few more minutes, they agreed they were done. They removed their blindfolds, saw their perfect shape, and cheered. They begged for another one. We tried a square, a heart, a perfect line. Each time they got a little better at working together. Our last shape was a circle. They took off their blindfolds and sat down.

"So did you pass the test?" I asked. "Do you think you are a community?" They all started talking at once. I held up my hands again to call for quiet. "First of all, you have got to speak one at a time. You need to listen to each other." Hands shot up. "So, do you think you are a community?" I repeated.

"Not really," said one student.

"Why not?" I replied.

"Well, we sort of had trouble working together at first."

"That's because you wouldn't listen to anybody!" a boy shouted out.

"Shut up!" she snapped back.

"Nobody was listening to anybody else," chimed in another.

"Yeah, everyone was talking at once and you couldn't hear the people who had an idea."

At this point, several other students jumped in with their opinions. Again, my hands went up, calling for order.

"You mean like right now?" I asked pointedly. Self-conscious giggles sprinkled the air. "What do you think, Rejeanne?"

"Not everybody helped."

"Certain people just took over."

"What do you mean by that?" The class started to erupt again, but I gestured for silence.

"So what do you think you learned from this test?" I asked. I expected to hear groans of resistance. But instead, students offered some thoughtful reflections. I grabbed a piece of paper to write down their ideas.

"We need to learn to listen to each other better." There was some giggling and then general nodding of heads.

"Some people had good ideas, but nobody was listening to them. Some people just don't feel comfortable yelling over everybody else. I think we need to make sure everyone feels comfortable offering ideas or opinions."

"We need to work together rather than against each other."

"Does everyone agree with this?" I looked at the group. "Does anyone think one of these goals isn't important? Or that we are missing something that is?" They all shook their heads. I kept waiting for the class clown (I wasn't sure who it was yet) to make some crack, but they all remained fairly serious. "Okay. Now we have a plan, at least the beginnings of one. We have something to work toward. We'll keep this posted and check in every once in a while to see how we're doing."

We decided to conduct small "community" tests on a regular basis, at least two or three times a week for several weeks. We did initiatives that were physical and required students to problem solve together. After each one, we would reflect on how well we worked together. We looked back at the goals we had set for ourselves and measured our progress.

Teachers frequently do one "group-building" activity to start the year. One student, describing his first day of high school, told me once, "I think in every single class we played those games like where you have to find someone who was born in another state, you know that stuff. That was their lame attempt at creating community in the classroom. Then the next day we started real classes." The clear message to students is that how we work together is secondary.

I have always liked asking students to set goals for themselves for the year. I believe that if students have to think about and articulate personal goals, they will be at least a little bit closer to achieving them. Although we had established goals as a class, I also wanted students to look more closely at themselves. In the past, I had developed a series of questions that focused primarily on academic success: Do you want to be successful in school? Describe one of your best pieces of work from school last year and explain what made it so good. What goals do you have for yourself this year, for example, getting all your homework in on time, reading 25 books, writing a poem? This year, I decided I wanted to broaden this conversation with students. I wanted them to think about themselves both as learners and as human beings. I wanted them to think about what they had to offer and how they could be better members of their community. I wanted them to be able to articulate their own strengths and to consider their weaknesses.

I began by introducing them to Howard Gardner's (1993) theory of multiple intelligence. Gardner believes that there is no single measure of intelligence but rather eight different kinds: mathematical/logical, verbal/linguistic, bodily/kinesthetic, musical, spatial, naturalist, inter-personal, and intrapersonal. We defined and discussed each intelligence. Although we all have at least some of each of these intelligences, often people have more of one than another. Mozart had extraordinary mu-sical intelligence, Michael Jordan's is kinesthetic. What about you? I asked. Which of these intelligences do you see as your strength? Every student was able to identify at least one area in which she or he was strong.

Each student then went on to do a "miniprofile." Instead of focus-ing just on academic strengths, I first asked, "What are you good at?" Students were confused; they weren't used to being asked this question. "You mean like math or reading or something?" No, I answered. Of all the things you do, what do you think you are really good at? Are you a good friend? Do you take good care of your younger siblings? Are you a good writer? Or reader? Are you a good basketball player? Musician? The next question focused on weaknesses: What do you need to work on? Being more patient? Being more organized? Being kinder to your younger sister? Getting homework done on time? Keeping secrets when you are asked?

The next questions focused specifically on school: What are your strengths in humanities? What do you need to work on? I wanted to em-phasize the point that, even in academics, everyone has some strengths. And, conversely, even those students who are very strong academically always have something upon which they can improve.

The next part of the profile focused on character. We had brain-stormed many different character traits: kindness, generosity, honesty, humor, reliability, to name a few. Students ranked themselves on a scale of 1 to 5 for each trait. They ranked themselves in work habits and aca-demic skills as well—self-discipline, thoroughness, punctuality; and strong reader, feels comfortable reading aloud, easily finds books to read.

I then asked them to review their self-analysis, looking closely at strengths and weaknesses, and to set goals for themselves for the year. What did they really want to work on? What did they hope to accomplish? They also had to articulate a plan for meeting their goals. What kind of support did they need from friends, teachers, their parents to be successful? Students responded variously:

> My goal for this year is to learn how to express my thoughts and my feelings better. I also want to be a better reader and writer. I need to believe in myself and I need everyone else to believe in me too.

> My goal this year is to have good writing machanics [*sic*] and creativity [.] I need good confidence and less negativity from my classmates and more assignments focusing on writing mechanics [.]

> This year I hope to do better in school and do my homework more often. I used to never do my humanities homework, but this year I'm determined to work hard. From myself, I need self-confidence. I need to know that I can do it. From my parents, I need support. They can support me by checking on my homework.

Some students wrote "I want to get an A in this class" or "I hope to do better than last year." At first, I was disappointed by these responses. I had wanted them to be deeply reflective, to understand the obstacles that got in their way, to identify a concrete plan that would empower them for success. And, in fact, some students were thoughtful in their responses. However, I have come to realize that, just as in acquiring any other skill, students need practice in thinking about their future, in planning goals, in reflecting on their own strengths and weaknesses.

As we revisited our goals at key points during the year, their reflections got deeper and more thoughtful. One student wrote, "The goals I wrote in September were kind of stupid. I was just writing what I thought you wanted to hear. But now [in November] I really know what I need to work on." Many students are not used to assessing themselves. In fact, some of them are downright resistant to it. "Why do I have to do this? This is *your* job!" "I hate this self-reflection stuff. It is too hard."

Anyone who has ever written a self-evaluation can attest to how difficult it can be. And yet, I firmly believe that it is a critical step toward taking responsibility for our own learning. *Ownership* is a common word in our vocabulary in the Graham and Parks middle school. Rather than relying on someone else's assessment, we encourage students to develop the skills to assess themselves. The miniprofiles were also a first step in emphasizing to students that everyone has strengths and weaknesses. They established a baseline for students to measure their own growth.

CHAPTER 3

The Parable of the Geese

SO FAR, 2 or 3 weeks into September, no one had asked me about doing a play. I was surprised. The year before, students had actually brought it up as they walked through the door of the classroom on the very first day of school: Are we doing a play? When are we doing the play? Can we write it ourselves? When will we start working on it? I knew I wanted to do a play again, but I was apprehensive about this group. Students needed to trust each other. They had to be willing to move out of their comfort zones, take risks, try something new. This group of students would need a lot of work before they were ready to do those things. There was little sense of safety. They protected their own fragile egos by attacking others'. Putting someone else down was a common strategy for raising one's own status. They built walls instead of bridges. I knew that doing a play would help to change those dynamics, but I felt we needed to at least reach a certain threshold of trust first. Perhaps the play could be the incentive to begin to work toward that threshold. I decided to ask them.

"By the way," I said one day, "are any of you interested in doing a play this year?" Some hands went up, but much to my surprise and dismay, several heads were shaking no. The resounding enthusiasm I had hoped for was seriously absent.

"I'd like to do a play," said Anna sweetly. Anna, a seventh grader, was a dancer and musician and had already had a considerable career on stage.

"Naw," guffawed Sam, a powerful eighth grader. "It takes too much work."

"Yeah," echoed a few other eighth-grade boys.

"I think it would be fun," chimed in Nicole, another seventh-grade girl.

"I don't," responded Randall emphatically.

"Well, we don't have to decide right now," I jumped in, trying to contain the damage. "Just think about it."

I felt terrible. Jackie and June were baffled. Our play the year before had been a huge success. In fact, each year, our plays had gotten better and better. By building the plays around the themes and content of our humanities curriculum, we had created a powerful way for students to make meaning of their learning and give voice to their own ideas. "Play time" had been the high point of the year, both for the students and for me. The three of us could not believe that kids were not interested. It would be June before I finally understood their response.

A few weeks after school started, I was invited to my friend Adam's bar mitzvah. At this alternative-style event, Adam's grandparents, other relatives, his school friends, family friends, and their children all crowded into the living room of the family's home. The ceremony was deeply moving. Both family and friends shared memories, observations, analyses, and words of advice for Adam. But the most compelling part of the ceremony was Adam's own reflections on his growth, values, learning, and hopes for his life to come. His theme was community. The audience gathered in his honor was testimony to its importance in his life. As part of his reflection, he read aloud a short passage called "The Parable of the Geese":

When you see geese headed south for the winter flying in a V formation, you might be interested in knowing about why they fly that way. It has been learned that as each bird flaps its wings, it creates an uplift for the bird immediately following. By flying in a V formation, the whole flock adds at least 71% greater flying range than if each bird flew on its own.

Whenever a goose falls out of formation, it suddenly feels the drag and resistance of trying to go it alone, and quickly gets back into formation to take advantage of the lifting power of the bird immediately in front. When the lead goose gets tired, he rotates back and another goose flies point.

Finally, when a goose gets sick, or is wounded by gunshot and falls out, two geese fall out of formation and follow him down to help and protect him. They stay with him until he is either able to fly or until he is dead, and then they launch out on their own or with another formation to catch up with their group.

I loved the image of flying in a V and each bird's creating an uplift for the next. So often it seems that "community" and "individual" are posed as oppositional. Yet this simple parable suggested that the relationship is dialectical. The individual benefits the community and the community benefits the individual. I asked Adam if I could share the story with my class at some point. "Sure," he shrugged and gave me a copy. I stuck it in a folder when I got home and wondered when would be the right moment to share it. That moment would come sooner than I expected.

Each fall, the middle school plans a trip, the goal of which is to build more of a sense of community. On a crisp but sunny day in the first week of October, the 80 students in the program as well as several staff and parents set out to climb Mt. Monadnock in southern New Hampshire. Although Mt. Monadnock is one of New Hampshire's more modest mountains, it is a challenging and rewarding climb, especially for city kids. It also affords marvelous views of the surrounding area as the entire summit is sheer rock.

We gathered at the base of the mountain to review the usual safety rules: Stick with your buddy, be careful on the rocks, be sure to fill your water bottle at the spring, stick with your buddy, don't litter, be courteous to other hikers, stick with your buddy. I had barely finished speaking when there was a mass bolt for the trailhead. A few students fell in the midst of the onslaught; others just laughed as they ran around or over them. The staff was mortified. We blew our whistles full force and somehow managed to stop the stampede. When they were all gathered again, I emphasized that this was not a race; we expected people to help each other; our goal was not to see who could get to the top first but to make sure that everyone made it safely and had fun doing it.

They set out again, this time at a more measured gait. People's different paces spread them out along the trail. Some kids were already huffing and puffing. Some were walking leisurely, enjoying the fall foliage. As I caught up to a group of eighth graders, I saw Troy. I knew he had planned to walk with Jash, but Jash was nowhere in sight.

"Where's Jash?" I asked.

"Psh, he's way up ahead," Troy replied.

"But I thought he was your buddy?" I asked again.

"He's *supposed* to be. But I couldn't keep up with him. He's into showing off how macho he is," Troy said with disgust.

"There's a bunch of them who just took off," said Anna.

I was alarmed. "Is there an adult with them?" I asked. They all shrugged.

I set off at a fast pace, calling out their names. After a few minutes of hard hiking, I got within earshot. They responded to my call and waited impatiently for me to catch up to them.

I was furious. "Where are your buddies?" I demanded.

"Oh, we switched around. Adrian and Troy were too slow, so we swapped with Andre and Damien."

"That was not the deal," I snapped, between heaving breaths.

"You just said we had to stick with somebody," Jash complained. "It was boring hiking with them. They were too slow. We thought this was supposed to be a challenge."

"Running up the mountain is no challenge for you, Jash. You're like a mountain goat. Your challenge is to slow down and help other people up. *That* is what is really hard for you."

The group was not convinced. They were champing at the bit to go on. Given how far back the other hikers were, I reluctantly consented with the stipulation that they had to stay with me. In no time, though, we reached the summit. It was a good 20 minutes before the next group of hikers even appeared on the horizon. As they approached the final ascent, the boys on top started hooting.

"Hey, finally!"

"What took you so long?"

"We've been here for hours!"

What started as supposedly humorous banter grew increasingly caustic and cruel as each successive group arrived at the top. I told them they should be encouraging their fellow classmates, not cutting them down. But my words fell on deaf ears and the chorus grew as more kids reached the top.

"Hey, EJ, you're pathetic, man!"

"Damn, my grandmother could climb faster than you."

In sharp contrast to our crew was a group of students from another school. As they spotted their classmates arduously making their way toward the top, they cheered for them, shouted words of encouragement, urged them on. When someone finally reached the summit, the kids welcomed the climber and offered chocolates.

"Look at those kids," I said. "Wouldn't you rather be greeted like that?"

"Naw, they're wusses."

Long before the last hikers appeared, the ones who had arrived first were antsy to leave. They didn't see any point in waiting around for the "slowpokes." Sit down and relax, I told them, you're not going anywhere.

The journey down was no better than the one up. By the time we got home, I swore I would never go on another trip with these kids. The trip to "build community" had had the exact opposite effect. The next morning, the staff agreed to call an emergency community meeting. Students were surprised to discover that their first-period classes had been suspended.

"What's the problem?" they whispered as they carried their chairs into the large science room.

"What are they so upset about?" they asked each other.

"Are you mad?" one girl asked me pointedly.

Once everyone had crowded in, I stepped into the middle of the circle.

"We need to talk about our trip yesterday," I started. The room became very quiet. For once, with 80 seventh and eighth graders squashed into one room, you could hear a pin drop. "The goal of our trip yesterday was to come together as a community and to have fun with each other. For a few people, that did happen. I did see some wonderful things yesterday. I saw someone sharing her water. I saw one buddy really encouraging another. I saw people who never thought they would make it all the way to the top make it all the way to the top. But, unfortunately, I have to say those were exceptions to most of the day. I want to share with you what I saw and how I feel about it, and I want to hear from you what you saw and how you felt about it." Without using names, I described a litany of incidents that had deeply disturbed me.

When I finally finished, I asked for their responses. The room was hushed. Then a boy raised his hand. He spoke hesitantly, slumped deeply in his chair.

"I'm not trying to criticize anybody," he said awkwardly. "But I did feel kind of bad that my buddy left me. I mean, I get why he did and all, but it still felt sort of bad. That's all." There was silence. Then a seventh-grade girl spoke up.

"You know, I didn't think I'd make it to the top, but I did. I feel real proud of that, even if people made fun of me for being slow. I still made it."

Another hand went up, and another. Students started speaking honestly about their feelings. They shared hurts and disappointments.

They also shared stories of kindnesses they had witnessed. One boy openly apologized to his buddy for not being more supportive. I was dumbfounded. I had not anticipated this kind of response at all. I had expected students to be defensive, resentful, or sullen. I was struck by how willing they were to talk about these issues. Few, if any, students had come to school that day hoping they would have a public forum in which to air grievances about the trip. But given the opportunity, they were remarkably honest and introspective.

The meeting ended with a challenge to the students. If they wanted to go on another field trip, they had to convince the staff that they had learned something about treating each other with kindness and respect. How they would do that was up to them. The staff did not want to punish them. But the message was clear: We know you are capable of something better. The student council would meet that day at lunch to discuss next steps. I left the science room feeling hopeful. The seriousness of the students' responses had restored some of my faith in them. However, it remained to be seen what their next steps would be.

When we returned to humanities class, I asked students to sit in a circle in the rug area. Once they were settled, I passed out copies of "The Parable of the Geese." I explained that I had come across this story at Adam's bar mitzvah. He had chosen it to share with his family and friends, and I wanted to share it with them. We read it aloud.

"What do you think?" I asked.

"It's a good story," said one student. Several heads nodded in agreement.

"Do you get why I brought it in today?" I asked.

"I think you're saying that maybe we need to be more like the geese," said one boy. Heads bobbed up and down again.

"What do you think?" I pursued.

"Well, we could help each other more," said another.

"Like on the trip," added someone else.

"It would be good if we worked together more."

"Yeah, we need to learn to fly in a V."

CHAPTER 4

Expert Projects

THE MIDDLE SCHOOL TEACHERS had identified research as a major skill on which to focus that year. Although our students were generally strong writers, they were not strong researchers. I knew from my own experience with research that when I was excited and interested in a topic, I was willing to spend hours reading, tracking down sources, interviewing people, pursuing information. But most of the research I had done in school had held little interest for me. It was simply an assignment. In the "real world" people do research because they really want to find out, discover something they didn't know before. If I was going to ask my students to learn research skills, I wanted them to feel passionate about the topic they were researching. Why not focus our research projects on an expertise we identified in our miniprofiles?

While I wanted to begin the year with a research project, I also wanted to challenge students' stereotyped notions about each other. The class was fractured into various cliques. Some students were clearly outcasts, actively rejected and isolated by the majority of their peers. Others were newcomers, particularly Haitian bilingual children who were just joining an English-speaking classroom for the first time. They carried with them a different label. Then there were the various social groups that had built high walls of defense around themselves. There were the "hip hoppers" and the "preps." There was the "makeup and boys" group and the crew that still liked to chase each other at recess. So-and-so couldn't stand so-and-so. So-and-so would die if she had to sit next to so-and-so. So-and-so would never get any work done if he was in the same group as so-and-so. In spite of my early efforts to build community through games and challenges, the classroom persisted in maintaining a balkanized character.

I wanted students to see each other differently. We don't see whole people in school. We see only pieces. Teachers, especially in the secondary grades, often see only a small slice of who their students really are. We see the child who is eager to answer a question or the child who can't seem to get her homework in on time. Students also see each other through narrow lenses. They tend to categorize each other quickly, not realizing that one is a gifted violinist, or another is a star hockey player, or that another has worked for years to build the strength to do an arabesque. I wanted school to be a place where kids could bring in more of themselves. I knew it would help me to see each child differently if I knew their individual strengths and passions; it would be enlightening for me to relate to them about an area where they felt really good about themselves instead of inadequate. If I could start my students off with something about which *they*, individually, felt passionate and self-confident, all of them would be more ready and willing to do "the school thing," that is, learn research and writing skills. I also believed that the students in the class would begin to see each other differently if they witnessed this passion and self-confidence at work in their peers.

As I introduced the Expert Project to the class, I reminded them that our theme for the year was community. Why look so closely at ourselves as individuals when we want to look at ourselves as a community? I asked, anticipating their question. The strongest communities are ones where people know what their resources are and how to use them. Groups are made up of individuals. How much do we really know about each other? How much do we value the skills and expertise that each person brings to our group?

I introduced the project to the class by sharing with them one of my own hobbies: quiltmaking. None of the students could imagine that their humanities teacher did anything beyond humanities class. But I brought in a number of quilts from home as proof of my craft. Though I wouldn't call myself an expert quiltmaker, I told them, it is something that I love to do. I don't usually think of myself as being very artistic, I said, but I enjoy the blending of color and design with making something useful for my family and friends. I explained how I had gotten interested in quilting and shared a little history about it. They were totally intrigued.

"Now you know something more about who I am that you didn't know before," I said. "I bet there are a lot of things about each of you that we don't know too. And I know, from each of your miniprofiles, that all of you are really good at something. We are going to do a project that lets us learn a little bit more about who we all are and what resources we have as a classroom community."

There were four phases of our Expert Project. The first was "Deepening Our Understanding and Knowledge." Even though students were experienced in a certain area or activity, I emphasized that they could easily deepen and broaden their own knowledge and understanding. I encouraged students to think first about what they did know about their topic and from that develop questions about things they didn't know. What did they want to know more about? Students were required to use a variety of sources including written texts, interviews, documentary videos, and their own observations.

The second phase of the project was "Documenting Our Knowledge for Others." I wanted students to recognize the validity of their own experience and have a real audience for their research. We decided to produce nonfiction picture books for third and fourth graders. Students were responsible for writing and illustrating the text. The production of these "published" books provided an opportunity to practice our writing skills for a real audience. It also gave me a chance to introduce and practice our protocol for peer critique and revision.

The third phase I called "Understanding Through Experience." People develop a whole different level of appreciation for another person's skill when they actually try doing it themselves. I remember watching figure skaters during the Olympics leaping, twirling, and dancing on ice. I calmly critiqued each one from the safety zone of my living-room couch. When I actually laced up my skates and tried to just skate backward, I gained a deep respect and sense of awe for what these skaters made look so effortless. I wanted my class to be actively engaged too. I didn't want everyone to sit in their safety zones. I wanted them to know how hard it is to do a basic plié, cast a fishing line, or draw a bow across a violin string without it sounding like nails on a blackboard. With recognition of the skill and effort required, real respect for each other would begin to take root. So a critical part of this project was teaching the class an actual lesson to "help us learn a little bit more how to do what you love to do."

The final phase of the Expert Project was "Celebrating Our Community Strengths." The class would paint a mural in the school that documented and celebrated the resources we had discovered in our own classroom community. I wanted to make a visible and lasting statement that synthesized our work. Through the process of working together to negotiate a design and to paint it, we would exercise our budding skills in working together.

Students were generally receptive as we reviewed the phases of the project. I had hoped they would cheer with enthusiasm, but, of course, their initial response was more measured. They had heard the word *research* and they were suspicious, guarded. I handed out an Expertise Project Proposal sheet to get students thinking about their topic and the research they wanted to do. Students began filling in the form: What special skill, hobby, or interest do you want to focus on for your project? When and how did you first get interested in your topic? How did you learn to do it? Why do you like to do it so much? As I walked around the classroom, I passed Marceline's desk. She had not written anything.

"What's up, Marceline?" I asked.

"I can't do this," she responded, her eyes cast down on the desk.

"Why not?"

"Because I'm not good in anything."

I was taken aback. I hadn't anticipated this problem. "What do you mean you aren't good in anything? You have mastered something that I have tried to do for years—and have never succeeded at," I said. She looked puzzled.

"I have? What?"

"Marceline, you speak two languages! Do you know how many people would love to be able to speak two languages? And you are an expert on Haiti. I know very little about Haiti but would really like to learn more about it."

"You mean that counts?"

I am still amazed by this girl's question. A few other students came to me with Marceline's dilemma—not feeling that they were talented or skilled in anything. Nearly all of them were bilingual students. Why is it that a student would have no sense of value for being bilingual? How has our society taken for granted and not celebrated bilingual students' incredible accomplishment of learning, relatively quickly, a whole new language—not to mention a whole new culture? How many of us spent years in French or Spanish classes retaining little beyond basic greetings and counting up to 10?

Marceline was not entirely convinced by my enthusiasm. As we talked about her project, she resisted the idea of teaching the class any Creole. But she finally did settle on a topic that grew out of her own culture: voodoo. She said she had heard a lot about voodoo ceremonies in Haiti and she was interested in learning more. Another girl chose to focus on Haitian food. A third decided to research the history of Puerto Rico. As long as it was their own interest and it was rooted in their own culture, I encouraged them to give it a try.

Students chose a wide range of topics: ballet, karate, metal work, pottery, singing, hip hop, fishing, ice hockey, basketball (women's and men's), baseball, baking, Haitian cooking, toymaking, gymnastics, painting, football, horseback riding, soccer, theater, beading, and violin. A few students who chose the same topic (basketball was popular) worked together; most students chose to work on their own.

We began the project by reviewing a variety of nonfiction picture books from the school library. We saw many ways to convey information in an interesting way to younger readers, ranging from *All About Whales* to *The Magic School Bus* series. We also invited a professional illustrator to class. He discussed the difference between art and illustration, showed us examples of his work, and shared some techniques and tricks of the trade.

Working from concrete models, we began to articulate clear standards for excellence. "What makes a really good picture book?" I asked. Their ideas came fast: It has to capture your interest; there should be evidence of a lot of research; it should show that you know something about your topic; the illustrations should communicate information in the text; one page should follow another; the words should be easy enough for younger kids to understand. Students gradually generated specific criteria for text, illustrations, and cover design that we then used as a road map to guide our work.

Another underlying goal for me in introducing this project early in the year was to use peer critique to raise the standards of the students' work. I wanted to introduce a protocol for critique and revision that we would continue to practice all year. I wanted students to recognize that by turning to each other and drawing on each other's skills and perspectives, they would find that their own work would grow significantly, thus infusing the theme of community not only into the content of the curriculum but also into our process.

So we began by talking about the purpose of sharing one's work with others. I pointed out that in the professional world of writers, artists, designers, architects, and many others, these people rely on other eyes to help improve their work. When we bring our work to each other, we are looking for support, feedback, and concrete suggestions for improvement. We discussed how it feels when we do get feedback. It can be very scary to make one's work public and to invite critique. Therefore, it is critical to remember that the goal of doing it is to improve the work. Feedback that is too vague or mean-spirited is not useful.

Because most people feel somewhat vulnerable when they present their work, it is important to first identify its strengths. Many people will ask, at this point, but what if there aren't any? What do you do then? Make something up? Absolutely not. Students are quick to recognize false praise. However, they are not always so quick (nor are many adults) to recognize the real strengths of their own work. Throughout my years of working with a wide range of student work, I have rarely seen a piece that did not contain at least one or two positive qualities on which to comment. Not only is identifying strengths important to support the writer; it also models and reinforces positive practices for the whole class.

So the first step is to give positive, and specific, feedback: "I like how you started with a question: 'Have you ever wondered about . . .'"; "I like the humor in the piece, like your play on words of *record* (as in statistics) and *record* (as in phonograph)"; "I like how you use a story about a boy and his dad to tell a lot of information about fishing."

The next step is to ask questions: "Is this piece about the history of basketball, or is it more of a how-to guide?" "I'm not sure when this story is taking place—in present time or in the past?" Finally, students offer concrete suggestions for improvement. However, we stress that these are suggestions, not "shoulds." If someone says, "The ending is terrible—it just stops and leaves the reader hanging—you should . . .", the message to the student is very different from the one received when the commenter says, "I felt really engaged in the story, but the ending left me hanging. One possible idea is to. . . ."

This protocol gives students some important messages. First, people's feelings are important. This does not mean that reviewers cannot be critical but rather that critique must be given in useful and constructive ways. This does not mean that we soft pedal or pander to lower standards; on the contrary, the goal is to produce higher quality work. Therefore, communicating honest feedback to the writer in a way that the writer can hear and use it is key. The second message underlying this protocol is the value of working with others. By inviting a variety of perspectives, writers (and others) strengthen their own work.

Response groups and peer critique sessions are not new to teachers. However, many teachers I know have struggled with making these groups effective. In the beginning of the year, students often beg, "Pleeease don't make me read this out loud to the class. Can't you just read it and give me feedback?" When I've asked why they resist peer critique so much, they generally give two reasons. First, they fear judgment. Most people who have shared their work with an audience understand these fears. I always tell my students about my own first experience with reading my writing aloud to a small response group of peers. My hands shook so badly I could barely see the blurred words on the paper. I was sweating so profusely that I could feel rivulets of water running down my arms. My voice shook. I was terrified. However, much to my amazement, people listened respectfully and then began pointing out things they liked in the piece. I was so won over by their respectful attention and so trusting in their good will that I found myself inviting and even pushing for critique.

The second issue students have raised with peer critique is that it isn't always very useful to them. Too often, students give vague and unconstructive feedback. "You need to work on your ending" or "That was good" doesn't give the author much to go on. Feedback needs to be specific and constructive. But students don't always have either the analytical skills or the vocabulary to give good critique. We need to teach them these things. When we can create a safe and respectful climate that honors high-quality work by taking it seriously, students will be much more willing to take risks and stretch themselves beyond their familiar boundaries. Then real learning happens. However, this respectful *climate* does *not* just happen; we have to work deliberately to create it.

I began by modeling the critique protocol with a few pages I had made up on quiltmaking. My artistic skills are extremely limited, and I made some deliberate errors in the text. Students had to refer to the criteria we had generated to analyze my text. We reviewed the protocol and I then invited the class to give feedback. Hands shot into the air immediately. Kids love being able to practice on their teachers.

"Your first paragraph is really confusing. There are too many ideas all jumbled together," said Seth. Even though I had just reviewed the protocol, many students tend to remain fixated on the idea that critique means criticism.

"Wait a minute," I said. "Before telling me what's wrong, what did we agree to begin with?"

"Positive comments!" a number of students chorused.

"Why? Why are positive comments important?"

"To make people feel better?" offered Markie tentatively.

"Yes, that's part of the reason. We need to feel appreciated for the good work we do. But it is also important to be looking at our work for its strengths, not just its weaknesses. When you point that out, we all learn something about what works. So let's try again."

"I like your description of how to make a quilt. It is really clear."

"I like the illustration you have on the first page. It is colorful and really catches the eye."

"Thank you. Any other positive comments?" I asked.

By focusing on the positive first, we have articulated some important elements of creating a good picture book. Other students are able to see an example of good work and consider their own work in light of this standard. This helps to build their vocabulary of their trade. As a teacher, I find the practice of identifying strengths first has helped me to see my students' work differently. Too often I would just focus on what was wrong. In fact, I thought that was my job—to tell students where they had made mistakes. Although I do believe students need honest and critical feedback, I also have come to believe that I can do my best teaching when I see a student's work in all its complexity. Taking the time to point out what is right is equally as valuable as pointing out what is wrong.

"Okay," I said. "Now, the next step. How about questions?"

"What are those triangles for on page 3?" asked Randall.

I looked puzzled at page 3 taped to the blackboard. "Those aren't triangles," I said. "Those are pyramids. I'm talking about quilting during Egyptian times, so I drew the Pyramids. Don't they look like pyramids?"

"Uh . . . not really," Randall replied. I looked to the class. They all shook their heads in agreement with him.

"Okay, I told you I am a terrible artist. Could anybody come up to the blackboard and show me how to draw a pyramid so it actually looks like one?" I picked a girl who rarely raised her hand in class but who was a talented artist. She came up and drew an excellent pyramid.

"Wow!" I exclaimed. "That really looks like a pyramid. I think I can draw that. Would you mind if I copied your design for my book?" She shook her head, quite pleased. "See, even though I don't know how to draw, by getting some help from Case, I can make my illustration better."

We then moved on to suggestions for improvement. Seth's hand shot up.

"Your first paragraph is really terrible. It's very confusing."

"Okay, Seth," I replied. "I actually think you are right. And I don't mind your telling me the way you did, but some people's feelings might be hurt. Could you rephrase your criticism in a way that I might be able to hear it better? And give me some specific suggestions for making the intro less confusing?"

"Okay." He smiled. "I think you are saying a lot of interesting things in the opening paragraph. But I think it would be clearer if you gave each idea its own page."

"Great!" I responded. "Do you all see how that response is really different from Seth's first comment? Which response would you rather get—the first or the second?" Everyone agreed the second was both easier to accept and more helpful.

I have not always given as much time and attention to modeling this protocol. In the past, I would explain the process and then ask (and expect) students to use it. I did not develop the rules with students so they "owned" them. I did not explain the importance of the rules in establishing a climate conducive to collaboration, so they didn't believe in its value. I did not demonstrate the process with my own work, so they didn't have any model or opportunity to practice with it. And I wondered why students struggled against revising their own work. All these steps take time and time is a very scarce commodity in school. However, I now believe that we must invest this time in modeling a process rather than simply focusing on a final product. As the saying goes, it is better to teach someone how to fish than to give that person a fish. It is often easier, and less *time*-consuming, however, to simply hand over the fish. But if people know how to fish, they will never go hungry again.

Critique and revision became an ongoing process in the classroom. Students worked on several drafts of text, illustrations, and cover design, constantly referring to the criteria for "What makes a good book?" Sometimes they met in small groups and sometimes they would simply turn to someone next to them and ask for help or feedback. Because the picture books required diverse skills in research, writing, and artistic design, students started using each other as resources. The traditional hierarchy in the classroom began to change.

Sarah was an academic powerhouse. Usually a source of help for everyone else in the class, she came to me in a panic.

"I don't know how to draw," she groaned. "I can't make people."

"What if you didn't worry about making them look real?" I responded. "Cartoon figures aren't realistic, but they can be effective illustrations in a book." This freed Sarah to begin drawing for her book on karate. A few days later, I overheard her showing her illustrations to Regine, a Haitian bilingual student.

"I like your maps of India and China," Regine commented. "Why don't you make those X's footprints though? Then it'll be clearer that he walked all that way."

"Oh, okay," Sarah responded enthusiastically. "I don't know what to do for the next page though. Got any ideas?"

"What are those colors for?"

"Those are the different color belts you earn. They show rank."

"Oh! Well, if you draw them like this, they'll look more like belts."

We had set a high standard for our final products. It was a struggle, though, to hold to it. Students were forced to revisit the criteria again and again. Although they were used to doing one or two drafts, the idea of doing multiple drafts with clear standards to meet was a challenge. Students showed me drafts that I knew did not represent their best possible work: work with insufficient research, incoherent text, spelling errors, sloppy lettering. I pushed them to go back and work on their drafts some more. Several got frustrated and very annoyed with me.

"Isn't this good enough?" demanded Sam about his book, *The Real Story of Baseball*. "I've done a zillion drafts already!" The book had improved significantly from its first draft (which had been nearly incomprehensible). The illustrations were wonderful, there was a lot of interesting detail, he had used humor nicely. But still, the book did not hang together. It was lacking a focus; there was no unifying thread. I tried to explain this to him, but he could focus only on how hard he had already worked.

"What do your reviewers say?" I asked. Together we looked at a sheet listing the criteria for the text. Peers had rated the drafts on a scale of 1 to 5. "Look at this, Sam: 'Does one page follow another?' 'Does one paragraph clearly lead to the next?' Your reviewers are giving you only 3's on these criteria. Let's look at ways to make stronger connections between each page." Grudgingly, he went back to his desk, but by the eighth or ninth draft, the writing finally clicked in. Later that year, Sam wrote:

[My favorite project] I did in junior high was my picture book. I liked it so much because I worked so hard on it and in the end I had a great project. I also got the best feeling of accomplishment which you get after working very hard at something for a long time and completing it. This . . . is one of the greatest feelings I have ever had.

Sam was not the only student who discovered the connection between hard work and accomplishment. As students shared their work with each other, they were able to admire one person's drawings, another person's story line, and another's clever cover design. It seemed as if quality work was somehow contagious. It wasn't that kids directly competed with each other but rather that they inspired each other to push beyond their usual expectations.

Damien was a student diagnosed with Attention Deficit Hyperactive Disorder (ADHD). He was frequently the target of short tempers and derisive comments by other students in the class. Even though he was on medication, he generally had trouble focusing during group discussions, staying on task, and refraining from impulsive behaviors.

Photo #1: Chris reads the final version of his and Sam's Expert Project book, *The Real Story of Baseball*, to his third grade reading buddy.

Damien, however, was very excited about his expert book. His topic was a controversial one: guns. When he first shared his interest with the class, some students, characteristically, made a fuss. "You're not going to let him do that, are you, Kathy? What about the weapons policy?" I wasn't quite sure what to do. I wasn't entirely comfortable having a student with a serious impulse-control problem spotlighting his interest in firearms, but I hadn't yet seen Damien so engaged in a school project. I spoke with him about my reservations, and he assured me he would do the book and presentation in a responsible way. "Guns are not a toy," he told me. "I wouldn't want to bring one into school. You have to learn how to use them properly and only in controlled environments. That's something I can explain to other kids." When I checked with his parents, they explained that this was a serious hobby, that Damien went with his dad to a shooting gallery each weekend, and that he was well-versed in safety procedures. I decided to let him do it.

Damien struggled at first with his research, but then he got hooked. He worked diligently at his desk writing and rewriting his text. He did careful, detailed drawings, drafting and redrafting until he got his illustrations just right. He started coming in during recess and after school to work on the light table to get the lettering on the cover perfect. He later wrote:

> I think that the work I am most proud of has to be my Expert Project Book. This is because the work took so long, so many drafts, critiques, and just a ton of work after school. From this I have really learned a lot about my [topic]. . . . The most difficult thing for me so far this year is doing big projects and big writing pieces because of having to do all the drafts, illustrations, research, and typing. When I think about the work I did on my expertise project I see all the time after school needed to be put in. But after it was done, it looked wonderful.

Perhaps the assumptions most challenged about what students were capable of doing were my own. I realized how much I had settled for work in the past that was just okay. Of course, we all have those students who do outstanding work. But I am beginning to see that many more kids are capable of outstanding work. When I began to ask more of students, they began to give more. What was critical to their success, though, was giving them sufficient time to do quality work and concrete support and instruction to improve their work. Lots of people are calling for higher standards for schools these days. But few of these people talk about how teachers must give kids the tools they need to meet these standards.

I don't want to create the impression that this project was smooth and easy. On the contrary, it was often chaotic. There were many times when I too felt frustrated. There were days when I questioned whether this was the best use of our time. There were times when I longed for the safety and neatness of a textbook. There were days when I wondered if I was expecting too much. With some students, I walked a fine line between pushing hard on them and not wanting to lose them. Some students found it extremely difficult to work together. But we worked through differences in the interest of completing a product of which they could be proud. In the end, not every book was perfect. But there was not one book that did not demonstrate dramatic improvement between the first draft and the final product. Furthermore, students had learned some critical lessons. They saw that it takes hard work to create a product of which one can be proud. They also saw that, no matter what their innate talent at writing and drawing was, they were each capable, with

Photo #2: A display of the final Expert Project books.

hard work, of creating something beyond their own expectations. Finally, they recognized the value of turning to each other for help.

By the time we finished our expert books, I was ready to beat a fast path into the safety of the industrial revolution. It was November and we still hadn't done any "hard history." But the kids would have none of it. "When do we get to teach the class?" they clamored. This was the part they had been waiting for. They had spent a lot of time writing about what they liked to do; now they were ready to *do*. They were ready for "Phase Three: Understanding Through Experience." Two students in particular had already been planning diligently for their lesson. Anna and Meribah were ballet dancers and they were determined to shatter the stereotype that ballet was for "wussies." So our first student-led class was in ballet.

We cleared out the desks and everyone lined up in rows. Anna and Meribah, dressed in their tights and leotards, began with the basics: first position, second position, third position. But the class was stalled in first position as we struggled to turn our toes out to the side. As we moved into second position, several people lost their balance. There was a lot of giggling and a lot of groaning as muscles stretched. Anna then demonstrated a simple plié, gracefully dipping down, while Meribah pointed out how she turned out her feet, how her back was straight, her pelvis in line, her knees pushed out to the side. It looked easy enough, but we quickly discovered that it wasn't easy at all. When we tried an arabesque, students dissolved in laughter. But when Anna and Meribah danced, the class watched with awe and a newfound respect.

We baked cookies, made pots out of fimo (a polymer clay), tried to catch fly balls, played the violin, did cartwheels and round-offs, sang, and dribbled soccer balls. What was striking to me was the transformation that took place as students became teachers. Peter had had a troubled career in school. He struggled with some serious learning disabilities and seemed alienated and resistant. He was restless and fidgety. He tended to blurt out his thoughts or needle kids sitting next to him. But he loved to fish.

He was very nervous about his oral presentation and lesson. When he first stood up, he blanked out about what to say until we reminded him that he had some prepared notes in his pocket. He fumbled about in his baggy jeans and pulled out a fistful of cards and glanced at them. This helped him collect his thoughts and he began. He opened his tackle

Photo #3: As part of his teaching project, Willy demonstrates
the art of metal casting to the class.

box to reveal a treasure chest of exotic and colorful lures. The class was fascinated. As he talked about each lure and when it would be used, he began to relax. When he showed the class how to cast for trout, he moved with a grace and ease I had never seen in him before. That day, Peter learned the value of preparation, the class learned about fly fishing, and I learned to see Peter a little bit differently.

One of our most memorable classes was in hip hop. The boom box was set up, the desks cleared out of the way, and Regine stood in front of four ragged rows to demonstrate the "running man," a basic hip-hop step. She first demonstrated the step at full speed. She slowed the rhythm to half and asked people to follow her lead. About half the class picked up the step easily, but the other half was totally confused. Regine was surprised. She didn't see what was so difficult about this, but she broke the step down even further, slowing it down even more. The students who knew the step started showing off, doing the step up to tempo, and adding turns and spins. But then, somehow something changed in the class. The teasing and showboating faded as the kids who hip-hopped with ease started coaching the others. When someone would start to get the rhythm, the class cheered.

We were finally left with four struggling dancers. All four were students who were used to success in school. They were not used to laboring to learn something new. The rest of the students cleared the floor for them. A couple of volunteers, along with Regine, worked side by side and walked them through the movements. With this individual attention, they began to get the hang of it. Regine gradually upped the tempo until all four were in a groove with the music. The class broke into applause.

It had been great fun, but I was plagued with anxiety. Is this a legitimate use of time? What are these kids learning? I began to voice my worries while eating lunch with Jackie.

"You must think I'm crazy. I can't believe we spent 25 minutes this morning learning how to hip-hop," I moaned. "This is supposed to be a humanities class. I'm supposed to be teaching these kids something."

"Are you kidding?" Jackie responded. "Don't you get what just went on in here? There was such a feeling of community. For once they let go of their little cliques and judgments about each other. No one put anyone else down. Kids were helping each other. They were teaching each other. Kids who have never felt good about themselves in school were able to teach kids who always know the answers. They really wanted to make sure everybody got it. Isn't that worth 25 minutes of our time? Isn't that the point of the project?"

Yes, at least it was one important part of it. Students learned many things through this project: research skills, the protocol for critique, the importance of revision, improved writing skills, the value of collaboration, oral presentation skills. Students discovered their ability to produce high-quality work. They began to view each other, even if just for a few moments, through a slightly different lens of understanding. They became aware, at least briefly, of the richness of their own community. They tasted the ease of working together rather than against each other. I do not claim that through this project these students were suddenly transformed into a trusting, supportive community. Kids, in fact human beings, just don't change that fast. But they got a glimpse of the possibilities.

CHAPTER 5

Sameness v. Difference

THE STUDENT COUNCIL had been meeting for several weeks on the topic of "respect." They had had several interesting discussions among themselves but so far had not gotten very far with a plan to respond to the issues raised by the Mt. Monadnock trip. One day, the representatives were sharing their discussion with the class. Prakan was warning his classmates that they had to "be better or we'll never get to go on any trips."

"Do you think it is about 'being better'?" I asked. "Or is it about the kind of community we want to have here (my constant mantra)?"

"I guess it's about the community we want to have," Prakan answered dutifully.

"But you can't legislate people being nice to each other," protested Meribah.

"Or force people to be friends," added Chris.

"The teachers are never going to let us go on another trip," complained Randall. "We'll never be as good as they want us to be."

"They just don't want to go on any trips. This is their excuse." Sam looked accusingly at me.

"I think it's totally unrealistic to think that everybody can get along," piped up Manuela.

"I agree, but that's not really what we're talking about," responded Sarah, another student council rep. Sarah had been leading the student council discussions and had already wrestled with these issues in her own head. I was silently cheering her on. "You don't have to like someone to be respectful toward them. Of course we can't make everybody like each other. We just want people to treat other people the way they want to be treated. You know, be kind, or at least polite."

"Kids are never going to change," Sam grumbled.

"Why not?" I asked, rising to the challenge. Growing up in the 1960s, I had felt that I could change the world. And indeed I saw the world change. Though I am not quite as idealistic as I once was, I continue to believe in the power of one individual to positively affect the lives of others. But few young people today have that sense of personal and collective power. Their hopelessness, and even cynicism, disturbs me, and I try to offer an alternative whenever I can.

"I totally disagree, Sam. We can change things. One person can make a difference. You have the power to affect how other people feel. Let's try an experiment. As part of your homework tonight, I want you to do one nice thing for somebody else, something you don't usually do. You could say thank you to the bus driver as you get off the bus, or hold the door open for somebody, or offer to help with dishes at home. Just one small thing, and write it down on a 3-by-5 card. Then, I want you to notice how the person responds to you. Write that down, too. Finally, I want you to notice how you feel about yourself after doing this. And write that down, too."

"Can't that be all our homework?" asked Randall.

"Nice try, Randall, but no cigar."

The next day, students came in with a variety of experiences they were eager to share. One girl had smiled and thanked a store clerk as she paid for her purchase.

"You wouldn't have believed it!" Catherine exclaimed. "This woman started saying all this stuff about how no one ever thanks her and I 'made her day' and it felt really great. I mean all I did was just be friendly. I was amazed."

"How did you feel about yourself?" I asked, checking in on the third part of the assignment.

"I felt really good. I mean, it was nice to make someone feel good like that. It was so easy."

Another student explained how she had helped her mom out with a chore at home.

"Usually, I'm kind of lazy and my mom has to nag me to get stuff done. So she was real surprised when I offered to do the dishes. It put her in a really good mood for the rest of the night. And I felt kind of proud of myself."

Although most of the class described very positive experiences, a few students had some less successful interactions.

"I held the door open for some parents on the first floor and they just went through and didn't say a word," complained Imani.

"How did that make you feel?" I asked.

"Bad."

"Yeah. Maybe knowing how it feels when you don't feel appreciated for something can help us be more aware of acting appreciative when people do act considerately," I said. "But for most of you, it seemed that it wasn't all that hard to act kindly toward someone else. And it also seemed that most people felt pretty good about themselves afterwards. So, going back to our conversation of yesterday, is it so impossible to think that maybe, just maybe, we can make it different here in school?" I thought I had them now. But I was wrong.

"School's different."

"Yeah, I can't do stuff like that here."

"People will think you're a real wuss."

"Does everybody feel that way?" I asked in disbelief. I knew some kids were willing to question the status quo. If only they would speak up. At least I could count on Sarah. But there was a collective class shrug. They still weren't convinced.

While working on the Expert Projects, the class also read our first novel together. *The Giver* by Lois Lowry (1993) raises complex questions relating to our theme of community. What is a perfect community? Can we have both community and individuality? What are the underlying values of our community? Set in a futuristic utopia, the novel offers a place where all the ills of society—hunger, homelessness, crime, violence—have been eradicated through social and genetic engineering, and the elimination of personal choice. To avoid jealousy or inequities, everyone lives in the same kind of house, everyone wears the same kind of clothes, everyone eats the same meals. Young people, when they reach the age of 12, are assigned their role in the community by a committee of elders who carefully consider each person's aptitude and the needs of the community.

Students considered a society that would dictate their futures based on their talents and interests. I asked them to think about their Expert Project. Wouldn't it be great to do that for the rest of your life? They were not so sure. Jon said, "I love baking and want that as a career for some of my life. But I want to do other things too. I don't like being told what to do. I wouldn't want to always be baking."

"What about you, Anna?" I asked. "I know you want to be a dancer. In our society, it is very hard to break into that world. Wouldn't you like it if you were *assigned* that job?"

"I guess so. But what if I changed my mind? I'd want to be able to do something else if I wanted to." The class strongly agreed.

"But wouldn't it be better to give up some of our freedom of choice to be safe?" I persisted. "Or to eliminate hunger and homelessness? Does it really matter to you that you can choose Nikes over Reeboks?" Some students couldn't step out of their own cultural biases to imagine the possibilities of another way of life. After one particularly animated discussion weighing individual choice against the collective good, Sam declared, "I hate this book."

"You do?" I asked, surprised. "Why?"

"Because it is so stupid."

"Well, it is certainly different from our culture where individual freedoms are highly valued. But can you see any advantages to living there? Like never going hungry or not having any crime?"

"No," he flatly replied. "It's just stupid."

A few students did consider the price we pay for our individualism. Willy wrote:

> Jonas [the main character] has lived his life unquestioningly and all his choices were and still are made for him. He cannot make any big choices because it is not "safe." Maybe it isn't. Maybe we shouldn't have choice. The wrong choice could influence us the whole rest of our lives. If we choose to drop out of school, maybe no one will give us a job, and we'll end up working in McDonald's for the rest of eternity. Bad choice! But if we don't make our own choices, do we lose something? That's the fun in life.

But others were adamant. "I would never want to live there," Christian insisted. "It wouldn't be good to have your freedom of choice taken away."

In The Community, sameness is the goal. Difference is avoided as a source of embarrassment and shame. The Community had gone so far as to eliminate color. People had been genetically altered so that they were color-blind; they could see only in shades of gray. Students were appalled by this. I played devil's advocate.

"Don't our differences create problems? Look at the problems of racism in our society. Why not have everyone be the same?"

"That would be boring," they said. "Who wants grayness when you can have color?"

I kept at it. "If we all care so much about our right to be different, why do we ostracize people who aren't like us?"

"We aren't like that," the class responded. "We like living with lots of different races and cultures and ethnic groups. Hey, this is Cambridge!"

And yet, the kind of tolerance they laid claim to did not exist in their everyday lives. They drew sharp divisions about who was "in" and who was "out." How one person wore her hair or someone else wore his pants was of the utmost, and defining, importance. Some students smirked or rolled their eyes when certain *other* students spoke. This is not unusual for middle school students. Putting someone else down to raise one's own status is a common, if somewhat disturbing, strategy among young teens. Self-esteem can be fragile. The desire to be unique is undermined by a powerful need to belong, to fit in. Struggling with identity is a hallmark of adolescence. However, it is precisely because of this that we need to offer students a forum in which to work through these issues.

The Giver had triggered thoughtful conversations about the kind of community we want. How do we balance community and individual needs? Are the strongest communities ones in which everyone is the same or ones in which people are allowed to be different? Most kids in the class believed that diversity made a community richer, at least theoretically. But what happens when different cultures collide? In the final chapters of *The Giver*, Jonas decides to flee the safeness and sameness of The Community to seek a less controlled world. Although he imagines a different world, how will he really fit in? Can he simply shed the culture in which he was raised? What if the values of his new world are in direct conflict with the values of his old world?

Again, we chose literature as the first step in examining these questions. *The Light in the Forest* by Conrad Richter (1953) is set on the Western Pennsylvania frontier in the 1760s. A 15-year-old White boy who has been raised by the Lenni Lenape tribe is forced to return, because of a treaty, to his White community. True Son is repelled by White ways. He and his Lenni Lenape friends scoff at the stupidity of Whites:

> "I think," Half Arrow said, "they are all near-sighted. Do you notice how when we come upon them they crowd close to stare at us? . . ."
>
> "They must be hard of hearing too," True Son mentioned. "They talk loud though they stand close enough to each other to touch with a stick."

"And they all talk at once like waterfowl," Half Arrow declared. "How can they understand what is being said? Why don't their elders teach them to keep silent and listen till the speaker's done?"

"It is because they're such a new people," Little Crane explained. "They are young and heedless like children. You can see it the way they heap up treasures like a child, although they know they must die and can't take such things with them. . . . Their house isn't big enough for all they gather, so they have to build another house they call the barn. That's why you find so many thieves among the whites. . . ."

"If they shared with their brothers like the Indian, they wouldn't have the work of building a second house," Half Arrow said. "Don't they see the sense of it?"

". . . Have you ever noticed them on a march? What do we Indians look for? We look for game or tracks or how the Great Being made our country beautiful with trees for the forest, water for the river, and grass for the prairies. But the white man sees little of this. He looks mostly at the ground. He digs it up with his iron tool to see how black and deep it goes." (pp. 17–18)

The Light in the Forest raised a lot of questions about cultural biases. True Son was forced into a world in which customs and values were strange to him. Because he did not understand White ways and because they were different from Indian ways, he labeled them as "bad" or "inferior." Some students found True Son's cultural parochialism amusing; others found it intolerant. White ways and Indian ways were simply different; one was not necessarily better than another. It was difficult for them to imagine how True Son felt. I realized that they needed to experience this cultural dissonance more directly.

As many travelers know, people often don't recognize the assumptions of their own culture until they suddenly find themselves in one that is significantly different. We needed to immerse ourselves in a culture different from our own. Because we couldn't take the class to some distant, exotic land, we played a simulation game called BAFA BAFA (Shirts, 1977). In this game, the class divides into two separate groups. Each is assigned a new "culture." The Alpha Culture is very social, affectionate, and nonmaterialistic. It is also rigidly paternalistic with its members expected to follow a strict protocol of greeting each other by touching, inquiring about male members of the family, and playing a game (in which winning is immaterial). The Patriarch, the oldest male in the group, watches over and protects his "village." The Beta Culture values free trade. Their whole raison d'être is to amass as many sets of playing cards as possible. They have their own unique language to ask for the cards (thus the name BAFA BAFA). The culture values aggression and success.

The two "cultures" know nothing about each other. To try to get some information about the other "culture" before visiting, two or three observers are sent to try to figure out what the values, norms, and mores are of each other's "country." After reporting back to their homeland, visitors are then exchanged who try to fit into the guest "country," much like tourists would. After everyone has had the chance to visit, the two groups reconvene to discuss their experiences and impressions.

Each group sat with its "own kind." Although we had explained that this was just a simulation, feelings and tensions were running high. I started by asking the Alphans to describe the Betan culture. The words came pouring out:

"Rude!"

"What do you mean rude?" The Betans were up in arms.

"Greedy!"

"Greedy? We weren't greedy; we were just being good Betans."

I had to remind the Betans to not reveal the rules of their culture yet, and to refrain from responding to the Alphan labels.

"Selfish."

"They ripped us off."

"Yeah, they took advantage of us."

"They were so unfriendly. We were nice to them when they visited *us*."

"Violent."

"They have no values; they just want to win."

I then invited the Betans to describe the Alphans.

"Weird."

"Touchy-feely."

"They gave me the creeps!"

"I was having a nice time, and then, all of a sudden, Vonel threw me out for no reason."

"They played this stupid game that had no rules." The Alphans giggled to themselves as they heard these judgments.

We then asked the Alphans to describe how they felt when they entered Betan society.

"I felt totally overwhelmed."

"I was confused."

"Afraid."

"I felt like an outsider, like I didn't belong."

"I felt put down. Instead of responding kindly to my not understanding, they just walked away in a huff."

"I felt stupid. I couldn't figure out what they were saying. I know they were collecting these cards. But Mike came up to me and kept saying this gibberish like: 'Mafa Mafa Mafa.' What's that mean? Then he waved his arms around and went up to somebody else."

The Betans reported similar feelings of confusion. They felt baffled and disrespected when they were suddenly asked to leave. But they also felt suspicious. The Alphans were too nice; they suspected that the Alphans were really after something.

When I asked which culture was better, each group insisted that theirs was the best. Only one student, a Betan, said he would prefer living in Alphaland. I have done this activity a number of times and it continually amazes me how attached students become to their "culture" in such a short period of time.

We recorded all these responses on newsprint and kept them posted in the room. As we further explored the idea of difference and culture, these notes would come in handy. I then asked students what they had learned from the game:

> I learned how to accept that other communities are different. . . .
> It was interesting to see what the Betans thought of us. I think
> that although they seemed mean, they were having fun and
> following their rules. They have different and opposite values
> than us, and that's all right with me.

> This game was great because you could really understand about
> other cultures and how it is to be a foreigner. . . . I am amazed at
> the labels of the Betans: grumpy, violent, rude, greedy. . . We
> couldn't have been that bad. I mean, maybe it was chaotic, but
> all those words are a little bit harsh.

> I learned a lot by playing this game. One thing is never think
> you're better than someone else because everyone is different
> and the same in some way. I also learned it is easy to think
> something bad about a culture because it is not your culture.

CHAPTER 6

Skating in the V

THROUGHOUT THE FALL, I periodically mentioned doing a play. The resistance to it became less and less vocal, but kids weren't begging to jump into it either. Furthermore, I still questioned just how ready they were. Every time I saw someone's eyes roll or heard an exasperated sigh, I lost confidence in them. But I also knew that we had to at least begin experimenting. *The Light in the Forest* gave us an opportunity to play with some beginning theater techniques.

Because of the wide range of reading ability in the class (some students read at a fourth-grade level, others at a tenth), I was concerned that everyone was keeping up with the book. When we were about halfway through, I decided to do a review. We split the class into small groups, and each group was assigned a chapter we had read. Students identified the who, what, when, where, and why of their chapter, and from those data they wrote a two- or three-sentence summary. They then had to create a "freeze-frame" or "tableau" of the essential moment of the chapter. These would then be presented to the rest of the class, using the chapter summaries as narration.

Students huddled in their groups. The task of identifying that "essential moment" stimulated some lively discussion and analysis of the text. As students decided on key characters for their tableau, they deepened their understanding of who that character was, how and why each responded to that critical moment in a particular way, what the character's motivation was. The element of public performance raised commitment and anxiety levels. Some groups worked collectively; in others, either by choice or by default, one person took charge and acted as director. But everyone was engaged in the task. After about 20 minutes, we convened in the rug area for presentations.

As the group assigned to the first chapter shyly took "the stage," there were lots of giggles and awkward body postures. People were jostling and poking each other on the rug. I realized that we needed to talk about ground rules. This was our first "performance" with each other, I pointed out. Actors do their best work when they feel supported by their audience. "How can we show that support?" I asked.

"Pay attention while they are doing their scene?"

"Yeah. What else?"

"Don't talk to people sitting next to you?"

"Uh huh. What else?"

"Don't laugh unless they mean to do something funny?"

"Good. What else?"

"Clap for them at the end?"

"Yes. What else? Anything? Okay, then, let's see the first scene."

On the count of three, students assumed their "freeze." The narrator read the summary and the class, at least some of them, clapped politely. I looked around at other kids just sitting there. Jackie jumped in. "You need to clap," she insisted. "We agreed that that is an important way to show support and appreciation. So come on!" (Jackie would continue to play the role of enforcer/cheerleader during the year.) They clapped, with exaggerated enthusiasm, but the energy level of the class picked up a bit. The first group began to sit down, but I signaled for them to remain "on stage."

"What did we see in this freeze that was really good?" I asked the audience. One or two girls raised their hands. "Go ahead, Meribah."

"I liked how Chris was standing. He looked really defiant."

"Great! Anything else? Anybody?" A few other students offered concrete positive feedback. Everyone else sat by passively. I tried to contain my annoyance with their seeming lack of interest as I pushed on. "Okay, any suggestions for how this group could make their scene come alive more?" Again the same one or two hands went up. "Meribah?"

"I think Regine should hold onto Chris's arm. I mean, if she's supposed to be Del, she would be worried that True Son is going to try to run away." I gestured to Regine to try it out. A few kids nodded in approval. Gradually, others offered ideas for one character or another. After a few more minutes, I asked the group, on the count of three, to assume the freeze again. The improvement was startling. With a few minor adjustments—a hand put on a hip, a gaze directed somewhere else—the scene had taken on a kind of vibrancy it had formerly lacked.

Even the most distracted students noticed it, and, this time, the class gave them a slightly more enthusiastic, and genuine, round of applause. Again, as with our writing, students were learning the value of collaboration.

Students learned another important lesson as we worked on the *Light in the Forest* freezes. In one scene, as their chapter's essential moment, four students depicted True Son and his younger White brother on a horse, fleeing from two White men. To prepare for the scene, they pulled two chairs closely together in the foreground and had two separate chairs in the "distance." Sam and Marisol, playing the pursuers, had "mounted" their "horses" and assumed "chasing" postures. Prakan and Mendette took the front "horses," each straddling a chair backward. Mendette was in front. The class approved of their choice and appreciated the basic structure of the scene but suggested building in more of a feeling of fear and tension.

"Marisol, can you look more angry? Yeah, that's good."

"Try looking over your shoulder, Prakan."

"Yeah, and lean into Mendette. Hold onto her around the waist," I suggested.

They both looked at me as if I was out of my mind. A number of eyebrows went up around the room. I suddenly realized what I was asking them to do. A boy touch a girl? No, hug a girl, in public? In front of their peers, in middle school? No way.

"Just try it," I urged. There was a hint of sniggering in a corner. I turned to the class. "Look, do you think they look like they're fleeing the way they are?" People shook their heads. "So let's just try it. The goal here is to make the scene look as powerful as possible. I know Mendette and Prakan feel a little weird about this. But right now, they need to forget who they are and be True Son and Gordie. They're taking a risk to make the scene work better. And it is your job to help them do it, okay?" Most kids nodded; a few buried their faces in their arms. I turned back to Mendette and Prakan. "Are you willing to try this?" They shrugged shyly.

Again, on the count of three, the four riders froze into their poses. Prakan was leaning into Mendette, his face twisted in fear. She strained forward, spurring her horse on. Suddenly we could see fear, speed, tension, determination. The class broke into applause. The actors sat down, relieved to be finished. It was time to go, but I had something to say.

"I just want to point out that something important happened here today. We've talked about taking risks in this class? That's what Prakan and Mendette did today. I admire their courage. You all helped them by not laughing or making it harder for them to try. In the end, though, their willingness to take that risk made their scene much more powerful. Right?" Heads nodded. "When you are willing to take risks and we all support each other in doing so, you can achieve some great things. Remember that. See you tomorrow."

The student council continued to struggle with the issue of respect. Finally, in mid-December with the winter holidays approaching, the staff suggested trying another trip. There was a tradition in the middle school program of going ice skating just before the vacation break. With all the discussions, there was a greater awareness of the importance and value of mutual respect. Perhaps it was time to move from theory into practice. This time, however, we would be more prepared.

As the buses rolled up to take us to the rink, students were filing into the science room, our community meeting space. Two student council reps greeted everyone and then carefully explained the purpose of this rather unusual meeting.

"We all remember the Mt. Monadnock trip," Emma started. "And we've been talking for months about the respect thing. We thought before we went on the trip today it would be good to talk about how we want this trip to be. Like what would it look like if we were really being respectful?" Slowly students started offering ideas and Nierika wrote them down on the blackboard.

"People wouldn't laugh at you if you fall down."

"Instead of the people who are real good skaters teasing people who don't know how to skate, maybe they could teach them."

"People helping each other."

"Not screaming on the bus because the bus drivers hate that."

"Cleaning up after themselves. Last year I got stuck cleaning up all the donut stuff."

"Encouraging people who are trying."

"Being friendly. Like don't be hanging with just your friends the whole time."

The list continued to grow until one of the teachers signaled to Emma and Nierika that it was time to go. Emma urged people to keep in mind all the things on the board. She also explained that we would reconvene for a second community meeting right after the trip to check in and see how things went. Then everyone filed out and got on the buses.

What happened after that still boggles my mind. I couldn't believe that these were the same students who had so infuriated and embarrassed me in New Hampshire. The exercise of "visioning" the day had had a magical effect. Kids were respectful and cooperative on the bus. They waited patiently in line to rent their skates. They helped each other tie their skates. Expert skaters guided novices on the ice. Kids who had never talked before grabbed onto each other for support, squealing with laughter. One student took a bad spill on the ice. Before I could reach him, he was surrounded by several concerned classmates. As I sat with him on the bench to the side of the rink, at least 25 students stopped by to see how he was feeling. I couldn't believe it. I had taken the worst trip of my entire teaching career with these kids. Now, with the very same students, I was having the best trip ever.

I wondered if the kids realized how dramatically different a climate they had created. Some students did ask, "Are we doing good?" The teachers would nod affirmatively and ask them back, "What do *you* think?" "Yeah, we're doing good!" they'd respond and spurt on ahead. I saw kids laughing and playing good-naturedly and even helping other skaters who weren't from our school. I did see an occasional push or hear a teasing remark. But overall, I saw them make their vision a reality.

When we got back to school, we piled back into the science room for our follow-up visit. Again, Emma and Nierika ran the show. The staff had urged them to focus on the positive. For so much of the fall, students had felt as if they were constantly under criticism for what they did wrong. This time, we wanted to celebrate all the things they did right.

"Okay," Emma announced. "Before we went skating, we talked about all the things we'd like to see happen." She pointed to the blackboard. "Did anybody see any of these things?"

Several hands shot up in the air.

"I saw Mike teaching lots of people how to skate."

"Anna really encouraged me; she was so patient every time I fell down."

"I saw lots of people helping each other get up when they fell."

"I was impressed that people who had never skated before were willing to take a risk."

"This was a really fun trip. People were nice to each other."

"People were laughing a lot, but it never felt like you were getting laughed *at*."

These testimonials went on for at least 20 minutes. I know this all may sound a bit unreal and rather corny. I was thinking the same thing to myself at the time. But it was true. For one day, no one had had to be on guard. No one had worried about being called a "wuss" or a "nerd" or worse. By "visioning" their ideal trip, they had somehow created a tacit agreement among the whole community to relax. Perhaps by identifying concrete actions in advance, students could translate the abstract concept of respect into specific behaviors. Or maybe setting a goal for one day seemed more doable to a 13-year-old than the vague and never-ending task of "being better." Or perhaps those months of community meetings and class discussions were finally paying off.

That night, I went to a holiday party at the home of some friends. The father of one of our middle school students approached me over the eggnog. "What happened today in school?" he demanded.

"What do you mean?" I responded, slightly alarmed.

"Cari came home beaming today. She said you all went on a field trip and that it was wonderful! She said kids were incredibly nice to each other and that everyone had a really, really good time. She was so happy!"

The victory did not last forever. When school started up again in January, the ice skating trip seemed a long time past. But again, another brick in the foundation had been laid. Although no behaviors were permanently altered, it was a day that few students that year forgot.

CHAPTER 7

Exclusion Acts

*T*HE LIGHT IN THE FOREST* had inspired discussions about the possibilities for peaceful coexistence between diverse cultures. True Son had been caught between two cultures. Did adapting to the White settlers' culture mean he had to give up his Lenni Lenape values and ways? As I looked at the faces of my students, I knew that several of them faced this tension every day. Would they listen to Haitian calypso or American rap on the playground? Did they remember to make eye contact when with their teachers in school and cast their eyes down in respect when with their parents? Could they speak Creole with their American friends standing nearby? Did the girls learn to be assertive in math and humanities classes and quietly demure at home? By reaching back to the 1760s, we had surfaced some important questions about a multicultural society, community, and cultural conflicts.

Indeed America is a nation of immigrants, some of us arriving sooner and some later, and it seemed important to acknowledge this mutual history. "How many of you," I asked one day, "are Native American or have Native American ancestors?" No one. "Then all of you came to this country, or your families did, from someplace else." I then asked how many of them had been born in another country. About a third of the students raised their hands, most of them Haitian. "How many of you have at least one parent who was born outside the United States?" I asked next. Half a dozen more students raised their hands; they came from Portugal, Puerto Rico, England, Thailand, Haiti, Mexico. Finally, I asked how many of them had at least one grandparent who came from another country. Several more hands went up—Russia, Ireland, Italy, and so on.

I wanted students to make their heritages visible to each other. We began a small project exploring our backgrounds. Students interviewed their parents about their ethnic heritages. We then cut out life-size silhouettes of each student's head and they filled these with images and objects of the various countries that made them who they were. Some silhouettes were carefully divided up: ¼ Irish, ¼ Italian, ⅛ English, and so on. Others were more impressionistic: the Cuban flag; the black, red, and green of Africa; a small pin from Portugal. One student, partially of Italian descent, had glued various kinds of dry pasta on his silhouette. Another strung a necklace with an Irish clover pendant around the neck of hers. Rather than cutting out his silhouette, one boy created a striking image by coloring the American flag behind his profile, which was filled with images from Panama and Africa.

Along with physical images, we experimented with word images, too. As a model, we used a poem called "I Am What I Am" by Rosario Morales (1986). In it, she triumphantly proclaims her diverse heritage and defies stereotyped definitions.

> I am what I am and I am U.S. American   I haven't wanted to say it be-
> cause if I did you'd take away the Puerto Rican but now I say go to hell   I
> am what I am and you can't take it away with all the words and sneers at
> your command   I am what I am . . . I am New York Manhattan and the
> Bronx   I am what I am   I'm not hiding under no stoop   behind no
> curtain   I am what I am   I am Boricua as boricuas   come from the
> isle of Manhattan and I croon Carlos Gardel tangos in my sleep . . . [this
> is just a short portion of the whole piece] (pp. 138–139)

The students loved Morales's proud and rebellious tone, and she inspired them to declare their own allegiances. Tessa wrote:

> I am what I am. I am Haitian. I am the island of my beautiful
> Haiti. I am the rolling-off-your-tongue language, French. I am
> the broken up French language, Creole. I am the lovely city of
> palm trees, Port-au-Prince. . . .
>
>   I am Africa. I am the songs and dances of my African ances-
> tors. I am the stories of which they told. I am the stories of my
> mother and father. I am the African country . . . Senegal? I guess
> I'll never know if Senegal is the country of my people . . .
>
>   I ring with the songs of Haiti. I move with the dances of
> Africa. I am surrounded with the opportunities of America. I am
> the hopes of our dangerous streets and struggling teenagers. I
> am the future. I am what I am. Accept it, or get off my back!
> [partial text]

And Seth declared:

I am not what I am.   I am Portuguese-Brazilian from my
streets and Haitian from friends   and Mexican from bur-
ritos   And I don't feel very Scottish Irish English Dutch
Canadian but maybe I am   And maybe I smile at the old Irish
guy smiling because it's my genetics   But old Irish guy is
categorizing, I guess   And maybe I'm not what I am   But
sometimes the Scottish part of me protrudes from my 100% All-
American blonde electronic blue-jean-clad technicolor rock and
roll 12–year old shell   And when it does protrude I'm red-
faced, fighting O'Donnell and Ryley and Duart pronounced
Duuuuw-ert and malt and barley . . . [partial text]

I was struck by the energy students had for this little project. One
girl who had struggled all year with homework brought in an exquis-
itely detailed silhouette. This was the first time she had completed an
assignment on time. She beamed as other students gathered around her
desk and admired the intricacies of her work. (Her parents later framed
the silhouette and hung it in their living room.) We displayed the
silhouettes and their accompanying poems in the hallway. Students
could literally see the wealth of cultures represented in our classroom.

This provided a perfect segue into our unit on newcomers to America.
My plan was to compare and contrast the experiences of three different
groups of people who came to the United States: the Irish, the Chinese,
and West Africans. We began with the Irish by using a computer-based
simulation project developed by Project Zero at Harvard University
called *Immigrant 1850* (Walters, Veenema, Pace, & Meyaard, 1990).
Drawing on historical information compiled in a database, students
"adopted" an immigrant family and had to find them a place to work
and live, purchase their food and clothing, and balance their family
budget. We read both primary and secondary accounts of the living
conditions and social, economic, and political issues of the time. Taking
on the voice of one member of their Irish families, students kept a diary
documenting their experiences leaving Ireland, crossing the Atlantic,
arriving in Boston, and starting a new life. Although they were encouraged to use their imaginations, students always had to remain true to
the data they had and to the history they were learning. For example,
if Patrick O'Leary had left Ireland as an unskilled laborer (as registered
on the ship's passenger list), he could not land a job as a store clerk once

he arrived in Boston. Nor could he even get a job as a day laborer if there was the infamous warning that "No Irish Need Apply."

My students, who were fairly well-versed in the legends of the civil rights movement, were quite surprised that other people, especially White people (although many Americans then considered the Irish an inferior race), had ever been the targets and victims of prejudice and discrimination. They were surprised to learn about the vicious mobs who vented their fears on these new immigrants and the political parties that organized to keep them out. Students were confused to discover that some of the political leaders opposing the Irish were also demanding an end to slavery.

One day, I described to them the New York City draft riots of 1863. The Union Army needed more men, and in July conscription lists were posted in the city. The war was unpopular in the city, and ethnic and class tensions ran high. A longshoremen's strike had recently been crushed by the hiring of Black strikebreakers. A disproportionate number of names on the draft list were Irish. Feeling unfairly singled out, an Irish mob erupted in anger. Although they first attacked draft centers, they soon turned their rage on Blacks. The mob ravaged Black neighborhoods and even destroyed a Black orphanage. At least 74 people were killed during 3 days of violence.

The class was appalled. That was so unfair, they said. People were so mean back then, they said. The Irish, of all people, should have had more sympathy for Black people. They knew how it felt to be dumped on, they said. As I listened to them decrying the lack of compassion and understanding in their 19th-century counterparts, I was struck by a certain irony. Some of the students who were most outraged by this lack of tolerance were the ones most guilty of intolerance on the playground, in the hallways, and even in class. Why did the Irish blame Blacks? they asked. I pondered the question.

"I think it has to do with stepping on someone else to raise yourself up. Anybody know what I mean?" They all looked a little confused. "You know what I'm talking about, I think," I continued. "Have any of you ever seen someone, maybe people in this class even, put someone else down to make themselves feel more important?" There was an awkward silence. I looked around at different faces. Tessa raised an eyebrow. Damien nodded his head vigorously. Emma shot a glance at Sarah. Rejeanne sat back in her seat, crossing her arms in front of her. I walked over to Damien's chair. "See, if I can just get myself higher than Damien . . ." I put my foot on the back of his chair and started climbing up on top of him. Damien, a little bewildered at first, started smiling as I struggled up, grabbing his shoulder, then his head. June and Jackie stared at me from the back of the room, a look of shock on their faces. The class, realizing that I was playing, started to laugh. I lightly placed my other foot on Damien's shoulder and, balancing unsteadily, waved my arms triumphantly in the air.

"See, see how important I am now? Hey, it's great to be at the top! So I have to step on Damien to get myself up here, so what?" Still perched on Damien and his chair and wobbling precariously, I asked, "So, is this a good strategy for making yourself feel better about yourself?"

"No," said Michael.

"Why not? It's a great view from up here."

"Because it's not really you. You're using someone else to make yourself *think* you are higher," said Tessa.

"Yeah," added Emma. "And you could fall off any minute."

"That's true," I said. "I don't feel very secure up here. I think I'd feel more secure if I was on my own two feet on the ground." I gingerly climbed down, dusted off Damien's chair and his shoulder, and thanked him. He was still smiling, luckily.

"Okay, I'll ask it again. Have any of you ever seen someone, maybe people in this class even, put someone else down to make themselves feel more important?" Several people raised their hands. They shared stories of various incidents they had witnessed or even been a part of, without using any specific names, of course. They discussed kids' motivations, worries, and fears.

"A lot of people are really worried about their image these days. They want to look cool, right? And they want to impress the cool people, see. So they 'dis' kids who aren't so-called cool," explained Rejeanne.

"I know it's mean, but it does make you feel better about yourself," ventured Catherine. A number of students agreed with her.

"You mean it really is an effective strategy?" I responded, feeling dismayed.

"Yeah," said Kelsey. "It's not like I'm really proud of it, but it does work."

"Do other people agree with that?" A number of heads nodded. "But then what does that do to our community?"

"It makes people feel bad."

"It feels unsafe."

"In New York City there were riots. People died. The need to blame another group, to step on someone else to raise yourself up broke that community apart. Why do we think it is so terrible when we look at that behavior in history, but we let it happen every day in our own lives?" The class was quiet, but thoughtful. "Something to think about, I guess."

My intent in this class was not to chide or lecture students. But I did want to challenge them to think about their own actions, their own choices. I wanted them to see a connection between their history and their lives today. I wanted to push the boundaries of their perspective. Students can better understand themselves by studying history. And they can gain deep insights into history by viewing it through the lens of human behavior, social interactions, and pressures. As David Hawkins (1980) wrote:

> History presupposes a recognition of the contemporaneity of the past and the historicity of the present. It is the knitting together of a story of the past from the life and evidence of the present, and a perception of the present as not only continuous with that past but as imaginatively projected into it. (p. 24)

Whereas the Irish experienced prejudice and discrimination upon their arrival in the United States, the Chinese were subjected to outright rejection. The Chinese were a visible minority; they looked different, had a different language, maintained different customs and tight, insular communities—and competed for jobs when jobs suddenly became scarce. The Chinese Exclusion Acts of 1882 were America's first official laws that kept out a particular group of immigrants. As the class studied the social, economic, and political tensions of the time, it occurred to me that the issue of exclusion was a powerful one for these students. Again, in the interest of connecting history to our personal lives, I began class one day with a free-writing activity.

"We've been talking about the Chinese Exclusion Acts. It happened a long time ago (although the laws were not fully repealed until 1943) and it feels very distant to us. But what does it really *feel* like to be excluded? How does it feel to be told 'go away'? I imagine many of us have had this experience at some point in our lives. Take a few minutes to write about a time this happened to you. Think about the situation, who was there, where you were, what you were wearing, how you felt, what you wanted to say but couldn't." There was no resistance to this writing exercise. Students dove in and wrote passionately.

> One day our class went to Canobie Lake Park. When we got there, I went for a ride. People were pushing in the line and cutting each other. I couldn't speak English very well. Every word I said some of the kids laughed at me. (Charly)

> Let's see, I don't really remember a time when something like this happened to me. . . . But now I remember when I was in third grade, I was the new kid. I had just come out of Morse School where I was the leader of my group. But when I came here I was not the leader, I wasn't even in a group. When we were out at recess, I wanted to play football. I got on the fence and waited to be picked. I waited, and waited, and waited. I was not picked . . . those jerks just left me on the fence. I just stood there. Stood and stood. Then I went to the stairs and sat there, staring at the tree, and looking at all the fun the other kids were having. IT REALLY SUCKED. (Christian)

> "How was your Easter?" my friends ask each other. Giving lengthy answers, they talk about all of the events that occurred. But I know they won't ask me how my Easter was. And I know they don't know about Passover, so they wouldn't ask me about it. It happens every year and each year it hits me with a pang of feeling left out. Like I have nothing to share but the reading of the Hagaddah, not chocolate Easter bunnies. (Emma)

> It was two years ago, me and my friends went outside to play kickball. It was summer time. It was a sunny day. The sprinkler was open and me and my friends decided that we were gonna go in. There were these other kids who started making fun of us because we're Haitian. They called us names. HBO stands for Haitian Body Odor. They told us we don't belong. [They said] why don't we go back to our country. They threw rocks at us. . . . It made us feel bad. I almost cried. (Marceline)

> I went outside to the basketball court. . . . I saw a group of kids playing a full court game. I don't mean to be racist or anything, but it's important to tell the story this way. Okay, so they were a group of black kids I didn't know, but they were around my age.

I just saw them as kids playing basketball. Not black kids playing basketball. So I thought it would be fine playing with them and they would let me play with them. So I crossed the street to go to the court. Then a white boy walked over to the court before me. I was quite a distance away from them, but I could still see clearly. The boy seemed eager to play with them. He said, "Can I get in?" They all stared at him. Looking at him up and down as if searching him with their eyes. The boy had on tight jeans and a white T-shirt. And they all had baggy jeans and no shirts on. After awhile they just said, "Naw, sorry, we have enough people already." To him, it was just a no, I guess. But to me, it seemed really more. Now I know that if he got a "no," I'd probably get a "no." (Prakan)

Their stories moved me deeply. There was no shortage of incidents to share. Each one captured a moment of hurt or pain provoked by racism, intolerance, fear, or just ignorance. Exclusion had suddenly taken on a new meaning.

I decided to take the lesson one step further. We knew how exclusion felt, but what did it *look* like? I asked everyone to move over to the rug area and make two concentric circles. The inner circle faced out and the outer circle faced in.

"The person facing you," I explained, "is your partner. The people in the outer circle are sculptors; those in the inner circle are the clay. As you know, clay does not hear, see, talk, respond, think, or move on its own. Each sculptor will shape the clay into a sculpture of exclusion. You have 5 minutes."

At first, there was a lot of giggling and silliness. But I reminded them of the power of their stories and the seriousness of their subject matter. If they were going to tease each other or laugh at someone's awkward posture, no one would be willing to take any risks. If they were willing to try, they could create something powerful. And they had only 5 minutes.

They gingerly started shaping each other. Powerful images began to emerge. Backs were turned, hands held up in rejection, faces twisted in fear or hatred. Students, a bit surprised by the intensity of their own work, walked around the circle of sculptures quietly. A few students were tempted to try to make the statues laugh, but I reminded them that the "clay" needed their support. The sculptures themselves worked hard to maintain their focus and concentration (it is not easy being gazed upon as an object by your peers without feeling a little uncomfortable) until the sculptors made it all the way around the circle. Then the statues relaxed. We all applauded each other's efforts.

"So," I asked, "if that is what exclusion looks like, what does *inclusion* look like?" I stood back and watched. Without talking, students turned toward each other. One put an arm around another, then another pair did the same, and another and another, until the whole group stood in a circle with their arms resting on each other's shoulders. It happened spontaneously. There had been no plan, no directions, no directors. Again they all looked a bit surprised and a bit awkward. But they also seemed quite pleased with themselves.

"Nice work," I commented, and again we applauded each other.

Teachers are under tremendous pressure to "cover" curriculum. The Chinese Exclusion Acts, if covered at all, are usually summarized in a paragraph or two in a decent U.S. history textbook. We spent a whole class period reading the laws, writing and sharing personal experiences, and making body sculptures. Some people might be horrified by this use of precious class time. Many social studies classes might have made it up to the Spanish-American War by the end of the period. But I believe my students left class that day with a connection to history. They had a different understanding of immigration laws and their impact on people's lives. They also understood that history is rooted in human motives and emotions.

Chapter 8

Making Connections

SOMETIME IN LATE JANUARY, students started asking me about the play. By doing small games and exercises like the body sculptures and the tableaus, some kids had caught the bug and were gradually converting the resisters. Every week, someone would ask about it. But *I* still felt tremendous doubt. When Nicole and Anna would ask, "Are we going to start the play soon?" my responses were vague.

"Uh, yeah . . . soon."

"After we finish our immigrant projects?"

"Mmm, I'm not sure . . ."

In spite of the celebration of the expert books, the experiments with respect, the successful ice skating trip, the historical parallels, and all the pointed discussions, the feeling of respect and safety in the class that I was seeking to establish continued to be elusive. Even when a discussion or activity seemed to trigger thoughtful self-reflection at the moment, it never seemed to last long. As soon as the conversation ended, students would be throwing barbs at each other again, rolling eyes, regrouping in their tight cliques. Trust in each other was tentative, risk-taking was reluctant, reminders of respectful behavior were constant.

We struggled with other issues, too. Fifty percent of the students were identified as having special needs. A number of students had attention deficit problems; others had severe organizational problems. I was constantly having to slow down the curriculum to make sure that everyone, or at least almost everyone, was keeping up. Several students regularly didn't turn in homework. How could we do something as high stakes as a play when half the class couldn't even meet a deadline?

I was beginning to think that maybe this class just didn't have what it took to do a play. Our plays had established a high standard. I felt my reputation was on the line. Part of my promise to kids had always been that they would be proud of what they created. I would not allow them to embarrass themselves or each other with mediocre work. But I wasn't sure I could keep that promise with these kids. I knew they had the potential for excellence, but I wasn't sure they had the commitment to it. I did not want to set them up for failure. I turned to my trusted advisors for advice. Both Jackie and June agreed that although this class had talent, they seemed to be lacking some of the prerequisites to make a play: respect, trust, discipline.

But each time I thought about not doing the play, I felt I had betrayed someone—the kids? the parents? the tradition? myself? I wasn't ready to give up on it yet. But I continued to push it to a back burner, waiting for some magical signal that would tell me the right time to begin.

In March, we began our study of the third group to come to America: the Africans. Using the book *To Be a Slave*, a collection of firsthand accounts of slavery by Julius Lester (1968), and excerpts from *Roots* by Alex Haley (1976), we investigated the experience of this group of people forced into a new life: the communities they left behind, the brutal passage across the Atlantic, the humiliation and pain of the auction block, the struggles to retain culture and identity, their fight for survival, the communities they created in the face of overwhelming odds. Although it is extremely important for all students to study the African American experience in America, it has an especially powerful significance for Black children. As Regine wrote:

> It is so painful to read this book [*To Be a Slave*] for me as a black person. . . . This book makes me think really hard about the past and about the present. I believe everyone should get respect not because of their skin or gender but because they are human. . . . I feel that we all should learn a little something from history because if we don't then the same things that happened back then will happen to us again and again . . .

Rejeanne, her sister, added: "I am so glad we are going to read this book. It is about time we hear the story from another side, the people who wore the shoes and walked in them."

Regine, Rejeanne, and other Black students' entries articulated a sense of exclusion, of having been left out, of their story's being omitted from the history books. The pain and anger they expressed about it was up front and personal. Even though the stories they were reading had happened 100, 200, even 300 years earlier, it felt immediate, close, relevant to them. Exclusion doesn't just have to do with who plays with whom on the playground. Or who gets included in a basketball game. One's story can also be excluded from the history books. These students were tapping into a deep vein of historical experience they had not had a chance to mine before.

The difference in reactions to the book between White and Black students was striking to me. Some White students found the book boring, others were repulsed by the horrors described. But Black students felt a deep, personal connection. One day, during a small group discussion, I asked students if they thought Black people responded to the book differently than Whites. Catherine, who is White, jumped in first.

"I don't think so. These stories are really sad for anyone to read."

Kelsey added, "Yeah, they are. But it happened a long time ago. It's not like I feel responsible as a White person. I think what White people did back then was horrible." Other White students chimed in or nodded in agreement.

"What do you think, Tessa?" I asked. Tessa, a Haitian American girl who usually offered her opinion freely, was sitting back in her chair with her arms crossed in front of her. The group turned to her. She hesitated.

"Well, I think it is really different to read this as a Black person," she started cautiously. "This book has been really painful for me. Sometimes it makes me want to hate White people. I know that isn't fair or anything, but these things get me so mad. Kelsey, you said this all happened such a long time ago, but to me it doesn't feel like that. These things happened to *my* people. It's really hard."

Why share this little story? Somehow something changed in that group. Some kids who felt their story had been silenced or omitted had a chance to publicly reclaim at least a little piece of it. They had a chance to say, Hey, we want to be included in history. The White kids at the table recognized that they could not speak for everyone in the class. They learned an important lesson about making assumptions. They realized that different people may have different experiences, feelings, and outlooks. They also realized that everyone's voice needed to be heard, respected, and valued.

Our discussions about race and racism did not dwell just in the past. Challenges to affirmative action programs were hitting the newspaper headlines and radio talk shows. As we examined the historical roots of racism and inequality, we had lively debates about discrimination today. Is racism a thing of the past? When we returned to our question about what makes communities work and what breaks them apart, it seemed critical that all people have equal access to education, jobs, housing, and opportunities to succeed. But do they? Are people of color still denied this access? Or do affirmative action programs promote a new kind of discrimination?

In addition to reading articles, both current and historical, one day the class watched a video of a *Frontline* episode produced in 1992 called "True Colors." Echoing the questions we had been discussing in class, Diane Sawyer introduces the television audience to two young men, similar in many ways—age, occupation, educational background, marital status—except for one. One was White and one was Black. With a hidden camera, we follow these two young men as they try to set up life in St. Louis. They look for an apartment to rent, apply for a job, shop for shoes and records, look at buying a car. The class watched, some in disbelief and some in anger, as the young Black man is repeatedly treated differently, with less respect and less access, than his White friend.

"That is St. Louis. That wouldn't happen here," said Catherine, who is White.

"It does happen here," Tessa jumped in. She proceeded to relate her own experiences with store clerks, which were even more disturbing than what we had witnessed in the video. Some White students protested that store clerks were just prejudiced against all kids. They'd been followed in stores too. Students, both White and Black, suggested that it depended on how you looked. Certain types of students would get followed, being judged solely because of their race or looks. But shoplifting was a real problem, some others pointed out. How do store owners protect themselves while not acting in a discriminatory way?

We continued to have discussions about race, discrimination, difference, and "otherness." These were not abstract issues to students. As they examined these issues through different lenses—historical, contemporary, and personal—these questions took on deep meaning for young people struggling with establishing their own identities and relationships with their society.

Each year, our seventh- and eighth-grade classes engage in a project called City Sites. For a full school week, each student is assigned as an intern to a workplace in the city of Cambridge. Sites have included day care centers, hospitals, City Hall, restaurants, museums, bicycle repair shops, community newspapers, Department of Public Works, nursing homes, and many other businesses and agencies.

Along with having the experience of working in the "real world," interacting with an adult supervisor, and gaining an understanding of the world of work, students pursue a research project organized around an essential question. This year, because of the focus in humanities on community, the seventh- and eighth-grade team asked students to investigate "What makes a city work? Are the City Sites interconnected in some way?"

Although students were expected to learn something about the particularities and services offered at a day care center, for example, we also wanted them to look at what needs their day care center had that were met by other businesses or agencies in the city. Students started to see that connections were numerous. Day care workers needed roads (maintained by DPW) to get to work, and many employees relied on public transportation. The center could not function without electricity and water (supplied by the city). The workers at the day care frequented a local grocery store for food for the children and a pizza shop next door for their own lunches. They counted on having the trash picked up once a week (by DPW) and bought arts and crafts supplies at a store a few blocks away. Students learned how, although the parents needed the center for child care, the center also needed its parents to be involved and active in the organization.

Though some of these interdependencies might seem self-evident, few of us stop to think about how essential they are. People tend to take their water, roads, electricity, trash removal, and so forth, for granted (until, of course, it is interrupted for some reason). What if no trash-removal system existed? What if there was no neighborhood park to play in? How would that change our quality of life in this city? How would life change for people in a neighborhood if their local pizza shop closed down?

As students began to see more and more connections, they understood better what makes their city, their community, work. They appreciated its complexity and the contribution each worksite made to the community's overall success. As a class, we were also able to reexamine some of our guiding questions about community in yet another context.

CHAPTER 9

Taking the Leap

DURING APRIL VACATION, I agonized about the play. I was obsessed. I had a knot in my stomach every day. I had to make a decision whether to leap into play production or not by the time we returned to school. I had never waited so long to start a play. The kids just didn't seem ready. I worried that even if we wanted to do it, we couldn't pull it off in the time we had left in the year. Jackie was doubtful. Other plays, with more committed and cooperative classes, she pointed out, had taken 6 to 7 weeks to develop a story, write the script, cast the parts, build the set, do publicity, make costumes, and rehearse scenes. There were only 7 weeks of school left before the eighth graders would graduate, June reminded me. If it had been hard to get them to focus before, how would they ever focus with warm weather, graduation, and summer vacation within sight?

But the thought of not doing a play seemed impossible to me. My classes had done it every year for the last 4 years. Teachers and parents were asking when we were doing our play this year. My panic was building. Maybe we need to do some intensive group-building work, I thought. I called a friend who had worked with Outward Bound and got five or six cooperative games from her. I seriously considered an emergency class retreat and wracked my brain for places we could go. Maybe I needed to just put my fears and concerns out on the table and confront the kids head on. Challenge them. Look, if you want to do this play, I would tell them, get your act together. I would be tough.

Then it hit me. If I told them all the reasons why I thought they couldn't do it, they wouldn't do it. I had to take the plunge as much as I was asking them to take the plunge. I had to believe in them so they could believe in themselves. They would learn to trust each other when they knew that I trusted them. We didn't need more talk; we needed to *do.* I had been waiting for that magic moment to happen, the signal that would tell me the time was right. But I'd forgotten that magic doesn't just happen; it is made. It is made when one is willing to step out of the safety zone, take a risk, and believe.

I shared my revelation with June and Jackie. They listened patiently, eyebrows slightly raised. In spite of their reservations, however, they were willing to be convinced. "Okay," Jackie said. "If you really want to go for it, then let's go for it. This may be really nutty," she grinned, "but since when have I shied away from trying crazy things? I'm in all the way. You can count on me." June nodded in agreement.

That next Monday, I wrote my agenda for the day, as usual, on the blackboard. After the "Daily Edit," the discussion about *To Be a Slave,* and checking in on their diary projects, I wrote "PLAY." The kids spotted it immediately (I was glad to know they read the agenda each day) as they were settling into their seats.

"Oooh, are we starting the play today?"

"Yes," I said, firmly. I said it firmly, but I was quaking in my boots. I wasn't sure what we were going to do about the "PLAY" today. I had no idea what it would be about. But I knew, from previous years, that somehow a play would emerge because we had dealt with issues all year that were real and profound in kids' lives. When it was time, I asked everyone to gather in a circle on the rug.

"Before we begin, I have to tell you something," I said. "I am really scared. You see, teachers like to have a plan. We are trained to know what we are going to say and do at any point during the day. But this playmaking thing we are about to begin is different. I really don't know what will emerge each day. We don't even know what the play is going to be about yet. And that is terrifying to me. But I have learned that this is okay. This is exactly the same place the other classes started with their plays, and they all created powerful pieces of theater. So I know that we will, too. We've done a lot during the year. We've explored ideas about community. We've talked about flying in a V. All year long, we've been building up our tool chest. Like the freezes from *The Light in the Forest.* Let's try to think of all the tools we have to use."

"The expert books—"

"Our Irish-African diaries—"

"Exclusion and inclusion—"

As they recalled various projects, activities, theater exercises, and curriculum units we had covered, I recorded them on a piece of newsprint. It was interesting to see what they remembered and what had stood out for different students.

"The sound theater we did with *The Giver*—"

"Our Irish families—"

"The 'True Colors' video—"

"The 'I am what I am' poems—"

"The parable of the geese—"

"BAFA BAFA—"

"When we watched Martin Luther King's 'I have a dream' speech—"

"*The True Story of the Three Little Pigs*—"

"*Light in the Forest*—"

"And *To Be a Slave*—"

"Immigration—"

"And affirmative action—"

"Slavery—"

Once we had our "tool box," I asked them to think about the product we wanted to create. What did we want to achieve with this play? How did we want the audience to react?

"We want people to know the kinds of issues kids have to deal with."

"But it shouldn't be all serious all the time."

"Yeah, we want them to laugh."

"Can't we do both?"

"This play should be about kids today."

"Yeah, the other plays had too much history in them. I mean, they were good and everything, but we want this play to be different."

"I liked the history stuff. It's fun dressing up in old-fashioned clothes."

"Plus that's part of what we've done all year."

"Some history is good; it just should be more in present time."

"Yeah, I agree with that."

I have found this exercise of discussing the play's outcomes to be invaluable in setting a certain tone. It allows everyone to air underlying assumptions. For example, as a history teacher, I regarded it as very important that the play have some historical content. Most students, on the other hand, felt strongly that their play should be (a) rooted in contemporary issues and (b) different from previous plays. These different perspectives, if not aired and discussed, could have easily derailed our efforts. By making them public and negotiating a common agenda, we avoided potential conflicts. But even more than that, everyone bought into the play because each student felt heard. It was not my play that I was making them do. It was not just their play either. It was a collective effort among us all. It was bigger than any one person's feelings or ideas.

By the end of the class period, the excitement was palpable. We had started our engines. But what was the play going to be about? What were we going to do next? How would we find that nugget, the kernel of the story that would grow into a script? Now that I had stepped onto the track, there was no turning back. I had finally gotten the kids to trust me and to invest themselves in the process of playmaking. But I was terrified. I was not really sure where to go next, and that can be a very scary feeling for a teacher. No teacher likes to walk into the classroom without a plan.

> April 25: I couldn't sleep last night. I dreamt about this. It is shaking me to my roots. I know there is great richness here. I know we need to find something in our study of community. What has torn communities down? . . . My fear blocketh me. All I can think about is what do I do? What do I do? . . . This morning we fumbled our way through. It was hard, it was sweaty. I was glad Jackie was there. I felt like we were walking into a dangerous swamp, looking for solid ground, trying to find the path leading us to—? somewhere.

I knew I didn't have the answers, so I had to turn to the kids. In spite of my panic, I have learned over the years to rely on their creativity, one of the most overlooked resources in a classroom. For homework, I asked students to begin keeping a play journal. Their first assignment was to brainstorm scenes, images, any idea for the play. The next day, there was no shortage of material from which to draw.

> I see a scene in my head that there is this one kid on the ground in a corner with his arm over his head for protection. He is surrounded by many teenagers about two years older than him. They are making fun of him and teasing him. The kid feels scared and frightened. (Prakan)

> I think our play should have something to do with the show we watched "True Colors" because it really shows the reality in our world of how people are getting treated. Or we can have a black kid and a white kid our ages be friends. The white kid's friends

think that he shouldn't hang out with the black kid. They say that because he's black, he is a gangster. The black kid's friends are mad at him because they say that he is forgetting where he came from and how blacks were treated back then by whites. (Regine)

I think we should really expand on the idea of exclusion. There are a lot of really intense emotions involved in exclusion. Being excluded makes you hate yourself. It lowers your self-esteem. Why does it do that? Shouldn't you be mad at the people who are excluding you? The people who do exclude are using power over you. Power is a strange thing . . . once you have power you don't want to lose it; you want to get more of it. I think in our play we should explore the issue of exclusion. The feelings on both sides, the reasons people exclude, how exclusion affects people. Also different ways in which people are excluded. It can be little things, a look, a gesture. Or big things like laws. (Sarah)

I really have no idea of what the play should be about, but I guess community because we did a lot of work around this topic. One thing we should have is something representing the geese that fly in a "V." I have no idea how we can show this. But it is something to think about. (Rejeanne)

Do you remember all the "I Am What I Am" writings? I remember the poem by a student in another school called "You Have to Live in Somebody Else's Country." I was just thinking that maybe we could have a school scene with all these kids sitting at desks, but all the audience sees is the back of them. There is a teacher at front writing on the board and calling on kids to answer questions. Everyone is talking and writing notes and fooling around except for one kid in the back who is the obvious "outsider." It looks as if the kid is getting smaller and smaller wishing he/she could disappear into the desk and then slowly the students and the teacher freeze and . . . the kid reads the entire poem. Then the kid sits down and the scene is over. The end. Maybe we could do something on the Martin Luther King speech too 'cause I really like that. (Markie)

I like the idea of having a sort of BAFA BAFA thing. Two cultures who know nothing about each other or their languages. And if we're doing this in the future, it could be aliens coming from another planet. And when there are different cultures coming in contact for the first time, there's exclusion. The aliens could be excluded from the normal people of Earth. The aliens could also be immigrants from their planet because of slavery by evil aliens. We could tie in so much with the aliens. But I don't like the idea of having song and dance. (Christian)

As we shared ideas, certain themes began to emerge: exclusion, difference, racism, fear of the "other," the desire to belong, the lessons of the geese. These were powerful issues affecting both our history and our daily lives, and they were rooted in our yearlong study of community. We decided to focus first on the things that break communities apart. Meeting in small groups, students brainstormed ideas for scenes and then improvised them. They also had to identify the essential moment of their story by doing a freeze, as we had done with *The Light in the Forest* chapters.

We gathered in the rug area. Energy was high. But the results of the students' work were mixed. Some of the scenes captured painfully real moments in students' lives. For example, in one scene a group of kids are "talking trash" about another girl. When this girl comes walking down the hall and stops to say hello, they all start smiling and acting friendly. When she invites them to go to lunch with her, though, they all suddenly have other things they have to do. After she goes off, the group once again starts "talking trash" about her.

Another scene features two boys walking home after school together. They are chatting and enjoying each other's company when a girl joins them. She starts an animated conversation about basketball with one of the boys. The other one, however, doesn't really understand what they are talking about. All his attempts to join the conversation are ignored, or at least not noticed. In the end, he finally gives up and sadly goes his separate way alone.

In another scene, a White girl enters a record store and is greeted warmly by the storekeeper. Shortly after that, two Black boys enter the store. As they browse through the merchandise, the storekeeper hovers around them suspiciously. Because he is tailing the two boys, he fails to see the girl steal a CD and leave the store. When he notices the CD is missing, he accuses the boys of shoplifting.

These scenes poignantly portrayed the injuries young people can experience on a day-to-day basis. They evoked empathy for the "victim" and challenged the audience to think about the ways we have hurt others, sometimes without even intending to do so. But there were other scenes presented that reinforced the very sense of hurt, exclusion, and powerlessness that we were trying to address. In one of these, three students are talking about having a party. When Damien walks in, they all stop talking. Tessa makes a feeble attempt to be friendly, but the other two quickly shoot her looks that shut her down. Damien gets the message that he is not wanted and is left standing alone as the others walk off the "stage" whispering "You don't want to be like him, do you?" The scene was powerful and definitely portrayed an authentic issue. But it was also deeply disturbing because these were the same roles these students played in real life in school. Damien was always the outcast, the oddball. This was not acting or taking on a character. They were being themselves. I realized I could not allow Damien to be set up that way and reinjured yet again.

Another group reenacted a controversial incident that had happened earlier in the year. At one of the school dances, a group of seventh graders had started playing "Duck-Duck-Goose" on one side of the gym. The eighth graders, who were interested in slow dancing, were appalled. They felt the seventh graders were acting immaturely and were spoiling the atmosphere of the dance. When the group recreated this scene in their skit, they did it in a way that clearly mocked the seventh graders. Although the group that presented it was mixed (two seventh and two eighth graders), the power dynamics in the group were quite imbalanced. I did not want to chastise them, but it seemed that they used the skit as an opportunity to put people down again rather than to provide insight into why people use their power that way. I decided to ask a few questions.

"So what is this skit really trying to show?"

Catherine, an eighth grader, was the leader of the group. "We're showing how the community broke down because the two groups couldn't get along."

"Hmm, I see. Let me ask you something. Who has the power in this scene? Is it balanced?"

"Not really . . . I guess I have it."

"You mean your character?"

"Yeah."

"How does your character use her power?" I turned to the rest of the class. "What are we seeing in this scene?"

A seventh-grade girl spoke up. "Well, Catherine's character is kind of using her power to put Mike and Peter down." Other heads nodded in silent agreement.

"What do you think Mike and Peter might be feeling? How can they show that?" The class began to make suggestions for revision and we asked the group to run the scene again. This time, the motives of the eighth graders were exposed for what they really were, an attempt to make themselves feel superior by putting someone else down. I felt we had managed to turn around a potentially harmful situation. Catherine, who in reality did hold a lot of power in the class over other students, had been defused without embarrassment or humiliation.

Another group presented something more akin to a body sculpture than a scene. Two boys got down on hands and knees while two girls perched on top of them, creating something of a pyramid. As they tried to hold their positions, Emma talked about how people step on each other to make themselves higher (a rather literal reenactment of our discussion of the New York City draft riots). Before the class could respond, the pyramid crumbled and all four students started bickering. Christian accused the girls of being bossy. Rodney declared that the whole idea was "stupid." The two girls turned on each other. Then other members of the class jumped in, saying the group hadn't followed the assignment. "You were supposed to do a skit; that wasn't a skit." With some difficulty, I called the class to order. "You are doing it again," I said. "This is exactly what we've been talking about. This isn't flying in a V. You're right, they didn't follow the assignment exactly. But that's okay. They tried something different. What can we learn from it? What is there that we might want to use?"

After each presentation, I asked the audience to analyze what had worked in the scene. By identifying successful practices on stage, we defined standards and criteria for good theater. We also acknowledged each group's ideas and efforts. We then critiqued each freeze or tableau (as we had in our writing all year), offering suggestions—moving an eyebrow, leaning away from someone, tilting a head ever so slightly—for bringing it more alive. Some students enthusiastically engaged in this process. But others offered little feedback. Some grew bored quickly ("When do we get to do *our* skit?"), and still others seemed more interested in poking each other than in crafting a scene. I was worried.

April 26: The group [my first section] went beautifully this morning. They worked together well. They supported each other. Their skits were wonderful. And then came the [second] group. Scattered, unfocused, fooling around. And yet they are very talented. Maybe it was just today. I don't know. But it isn't at all clear to me what the next step is.

But I was surprised when I read the students' journals the next day.

I really liked what we did today. It was really fun. I got touched when I saw Markie standing there alone when everybody left her. The look on her face was really good. I can't wait for tomorrow. (Prakan)

Today we made skits. I liked doing it. I think that ours was good, and I can't wait to do it. I have never really done many plays, but I like acting and doing skits when I really get into it. (Willy)

I really thought this was a great second day of working on the play. I think our play should have something to do with discrimination and the quick skits are really powerful. They make you think twice before you do something to another person. (Regine)

CHAPTER 10

Warm-ups

MOST OF THE KIDS were on board. They wanted to make a play. But they still didn't realize the concentration and discipline it really required. The next day, before any talking, presenting, or critiquing, I introduced a warm-up routine. Every time we worked on the play, we began with this routine. In a large circle, we would begin with a simple clapping game. Standing in the center of the circle, I would clap my hands in a wide arc over my head. As in the "Simon Says" game, students would join in the motion and rhythm. The trick was to pay attention to when I stopped. If someone wasn't paying attention, he or she would announce it to the class with a loud clap. In past years, it had generally taken two or three attempts before everyone was really focused. This year, the norm was five or six attempts. On a bad day, it could be up to 10 or 12.

After clapping, we would go through a series of stretches: shoulders, arms, fingers; hips, legs, toes. We would gently rotate our heads, drop down to touch our toes and slowly roll up, one vertebra at a time, to standing position. We scrunched up our faces like Cabbage Patch dolls ("lemon faces," I called them) and roared like lions. We silently mouthed our vowels, exaggerating each one, and then slowly built up to a deafening chant: *A E I O U*!

Although the physical act of stretching out was useful, the real value of the warm-up routine was its ritual. Forming the circle with the clapping game signaled a transition; "Play Time" had arrived. It demanded participation and involvement. Students could not just come in the room, slump down at their desks, and be passive. It called on all students to bring their attention, concentration, and energy to bear on the task of making theater together. It also shook kids out of their "comfort zones" and loosened up the binds of looking cool. Trying to scrunch one's face into a lemonpuss isn't an activity that can make anyone look very cool. It pushed kids into taking risks, albeit tiny ones. But, as I would say to them each day, if we can't experiment in the safety of a warm-up circle, how will we ever do anything impressive on a public stage?

Each day, after warm-ups and before working on the story of the play, we tried various theater games and activities. In pairs, we "mirrored" each other's movement in slow motion, trying to move as one organism, blurring the lines between leader and follower. Although this activity may seem simple, tremendous focus and concentration are required to do it well. Young adolescents can find it very difficult just to look someone in the eye. The first time we tried it, several students dissolved in giggles. Others tried to trick their partners with sudden movement. One student was so threatened by this activity, he walked out of the room the first time we tried it. But we kept at it. We took turns watching each other, and gradually the pairs that moved with grace and fluidity inspired the others. Once we mastered mirroring in pairs, we tried it in groups of four and then groups of six.

One day, we tried "flocking." I had been attending a series of theater workshops for teachers sponsored by the Cambridge School Department. One afternoon, I was describing my class to the workshop leader, John Bay of the Studebaker Theatre Company, explaining how we had been exploring the theme of community all year and were trying to create an original play that brought together all the threads of our study. When I told John about the parable of the geese and flying in a V, he responded excitedly, "Oh, I love the image of the geese flying in a V. That image could run through the entire play. Have you ever tried flocking? It's perfect for you!" To "flock," I discovered, you need a fairly large group of people. You make a shape like a baseball diamond, with one person at each of the bases and everyone else filling in the middle, all facing in one direction. The person at home plate begins moving in slow motion and the rest of the "flock" follows, moving in the same way. As in mirroring, the goal is to look like one single organism. When the leader turns her body toward first base, the person there, without interrupting the flow of the movement, takes over leadership of the "flock." In this way, the leadership, as in the parable of the geese, is passed around the bases.

I couldn't wait to try this with the kids. Without explaining what we were going to do, I asked for three volunteers to be the bases (I was home plate). I picked two girls and a boy. Because of the cramped space of the classroom, I split the class in half. One group of nine spread out in the middle of the diamond; the other group formed an outer circle to watch. I then explained what we were going to do, how the leadership would be passed, and our goal: to move as one. I began moving slowly, stretching my arms high over my head, letting them drop slowly, bending at the waist to the right, dipping down toward the floor. The kids followed pretty well, and I "threw" the lead to Meribah. A ballet dancer, she was in her element. She moved gracefully and then passed the lead on to Manuela. Manuela was a gymnast, and she too glided through the movement. But as she moved toward third base, Sam looked apprehensive. His movement was jerky and stifled. "I can't think of anything to do," he moaned.

"Don't think about it," I counseled. "Just let your body take over."

"This isn't working," he responded, and then stopped.

"Okay," I said. "I know this might feel a little weird for some of you. But don't give up. Sam, you're an athlete. Take some of your sports moves, pretend you're at bat or throwing a pitch or taking a free throw, and just do it in slow-motion."

"Okay," he said doubtfully and began again. This time he moved with more comfort and confidence. We went around the bases a second time. This time, I could feel their concentration. The synchronicity of movement was mesmerizing. When we finally came to rest, the observers burst into applause.

"That was so cool!"

"You guys looked great!"

"You were really together!"

The groups switched places and this time I was able to witness how this exercise captured physically the power of community. Not only did it demonstrate that power to observers, but also it created it among the participants as each student sought the rhythm of the flock.

I also wanted kids to open up their voices. At another drama workshop, we had tried chanting. Like flocking, chanting created an energy, but this time through sound rather than motion, that was much greater than the sum of its parts. It was meditative and transformative. I decided to try it with the kids. *I am really going off the deep end here,* I thought to myself as we gathered on the rug area in a large circle. I prayed that no visitors would wander through my door in the next 15 minutes.

"How many of you have ever tried chanting before?" I asked. Kids looked at me blankly. "Okay, well, we're going to try something new today using our voices. I know it might feel a little uncomfortable at first, but it is really cool when it works. I can't explain to you what the 'it' is, but you will know it if you reach it. I like to do this closing my eyes; it helps me concentrate better. I'll start and you join in. As I said, I can't tell you what happens when it really works, but you'll know it if and when you get there."

I began with "ommm" and the class joined in tentatively. I tried to pull them in with my voice. Some students grew stronger, but I knew, even though my eyes were closed, that they weren't all singing. There was a burst of laughter in one corner. Several students stopped to take a breath all at the same time. The few remaining chanters stopped in embarrassment. I opened my eyes and looked around the circle.

"Anyone get there?" I asked.

"No."

"Me neither," I said. "Why not? What do you think kept us from getting there?"

"Well, I know I started laughing," confessed Mike. "I guess I just got embarrassed, so I started laughing. I think that made it hard for other people to concentrate."

"Other thoughts?" I asked.

"Not everyone was really doing it, so it was harder to sing. I felt like I was sticking out."

"Yeah, everybody was waiting for the other person to do it, so no one tried very hard."

"Yeah."

"You know," I responded, "if we want to make a play together, we need everyone working at it. We can't leave it to someone else to do the work. Well, we could, but then it won't be very good. The plays that kids have done before were great because everyone contributed. Other thoughts?"

"When you stopped to take a breath, I thought you were stopping, so I stopped, and then everybody stopped," said Emma.

"I have to breathe too," I replied. "You've got to really listen to be able to tell when someone is just taking a breath and when we are stopping. Now that we know why it didn't work the first time, do you think we could try it again? Is everybody willing to take the risk this time?" I asked. Heads nodded. "Okay, here we go." I started again, "Oooommm." This time, the sound volume was twice what it had been. The tentativeness was gone. At one point, three or four students stopped to take a breath, and the energy started to waiver, but others quickly filled in. The sound regained its balance and, at a certain point, I felt the "it" fill the room. When we finally stopped, I looked around the circle.

"Did anybody get there? Anybody feel 'it'?"

Seth's hand shot up. "I know this is going to sound really weird, but at a certain point, I felt like I was lifting off the ground. It almost felt like flying!"

Sam jumped in. "Yeah, it was really weird. But for a moment, I felt like we could lift almost anything, like that garbage truck out there. I felt like we had this power that together we could hold that garbage truck up in the air."

As I write this, I think about the people wondering: What kind of teacher is this? Chanting and flocking? What about learning some real skills? Enough of this touchy-feely stuff and back to basics. Where is the reading and writing? Can they spell? In fact, I have asked myself these questions many times. What am I really teaching these kids? Are they acquiring the tools they need to make it in the "real world"? Is this a good use of our time? I ask. Over and over again, as I challenge myself with this question, I find myself answering "yes." If that is all a teacher did, I would be seriously concerned. But that is not all we did. We did not neglect reading and writing and grammar and history. But I wanted my students to learn more than those things. I wanted them to learn about their power as individuals and their power as a group. I wanted them to learn to count on each other. I wanted them to learn to try new things. I wanted them to learn to take risks in learning. I wanted them to learn they could experience the world in different ways. I wanted them to learn how empowering a safe and respectful environment can be. I wanted them to see possibilities they hadn't thought possible in school. Could they learn this through 15 minutes of chanting or flocking? No. Not if we did it only once and then "got on with the curriculum." They would learn those lessons only if we made consistent time and space for those learning opportunities.

The first week of working on the play was tough. After the initial brainstorming and presentation of scenes, it was clear that we had a lot of great material and wonderful ideas, but, by the end of the week, we still had no script or story or even a specific focus. No clear structure or story line had emerged. The kids were growing impatient.

Personally, I think the play is coming along realllllllllllly slow
and that if we do come up with a play it won't be very good
because we are rushing so much. I think we need to cut down on
warm-ups and get to the real stuff. Because the warm-ups take
up about thirty minutes and we could do so much in thirty
minutes. I think when we are doing these skits we need to really
take action and get our lazy butts moving!! (Meribah)

Those skits and little exercises are really fun, but every time I
look at a calendar, I start to wonder do we have enough time? . . .
we really need to start planning the script. I know you're the
teacher and have done this before and know better, but we really
need to start working on it. (Prakan)

I don't really think we're getting anywhere. Don't get me wrong,
the stage games are fun and all and I wouldn't mind if we just
played them for the rest of the year instead of doing a play at all.
But today is May 2. We have one month to write, rehearse, and
perform the play and I don't feel like we're really getting anywhere. Brady [a student in the previous year's play] said that
anything we're writing right now will be the play, but I can't see
the skits we're doing unfold into a real play. (Kelsey)

Everybody in the class is scared that this play won't be as good
as last year's. (Christian)

They wanted to trust me, but they were focused on the end product. They hadn't yet realized the importance of the journey itself. But I
knew that we first had to establish the right climate and habits through
the warm-ups, games, improvisations, and critique sessions. Students
had to be able to listen to each other. They had to be ready to experiment, to share ideas without judgment, to venture into unsure, unex-
plored territory. We had struggled with these issues all year. I knew
we were making progress, but it was slow.

May 5: Well, their attention was better today. But I still don't
feel like we've got it. There are those who get it and those who
don't. I worry about the ones who don't. The creative juices
aren't flowing. Too many of them are not thinking or are not
taking risks. Argh. I want so badly to find the kernel of the story.
Where is the story going to come from?

CHAPTER 11

Finding the Story

TIME WAS RUNNING OUT. Because of other important dates and events, we had to perform the play no later than June 1. I knew we had to begin working on a script. But what was the story? We needed a plot. The first year my class wrote their own play we had worked closely with a theater professional. Diana and I continued to stay in touch; she was a constant source of comfort and advice. When I had struggled before with "finding the story," she suggested that I sit down and just start writing a plot outline. "Write as much as you know," she advised. "You'll be amazed at how things start to fall into place." That weekend, I decided to sit down and start writing.

It seemed as if we had three threads to work with: our theme of community and the lessons from the geese, the historical lessons we had studied, and the vignettes about exclusion drawn from students' own lives. How could we weave these three threads together to make a coherent story? I loved John's idea (from the theater workshop) of a repeating image of geese flying in a V. A few students had raised the idea that a historical time line should run through the play, an idea everyone had liked. And we had several possible scenes that kids had improvised. I began to lay out these threads—the image of the geese, a time-line vignette to inject the historical perspective, and a contemporary story about how kids treat each other—and gradually a structure began to emerge. After a few hours, I had a plan, a rough outline with lots of questions and fuzzy areas, but nevertheless a concrete plan to present to the class on Monday. I felt that finally a structure had emerged that reflected and incorporated the thinking of the whole class. I hoped the kids would feel the same way. If we could agree to the skeleton, then we could begin the process of putting some flesh on those bones together.

On Monday morning, we gathered on the rug.

"I think I've got an outline for the play," I began nervously. After emphasizing the collaborative process of building the play, I worried that students would feel that, in the end, "as usual," the teacher had "taken over." Or perhaps the story did not say what they wanted it to say. We just needed to be sure the story reflected their vision as well as mine. I was prepared for them to reject my proposal. "I've tried to take the things we've talked about and a lot of the different ideas people have had and put them together. It's not finished yet and there are lots of questions, but I want to know what you think. Want to hear it?" There was a resounding YES! "Okay, here it is." I passed out copies of the outline and began reading aloud.

As I was reading through the outline, I glanced up to check the class's response. They were listening intently; heads were nodding in agreement. They were hooked. When I finished, the class burst into applause. "What's next?" "How do we make a script?" "Who is going to write the actual lines?" "When do we get our parts?" Their enthusiasm was infectious. At this point, I realized that a subtle shift had taken place in the classroom. As a teacher, I have often felt like a locomotive pulling a freight train. The teacher is the engine dragging students along. If the engine stops, the train stops. But now, those lines were blurring. I didn't need to drag them along. We were doing it together; we were becoming a real team, working to make the best possible product between us.

"Okay, so you like the plan?" The class erupted into happy chaos. "Okay, okay," I called. "Let's make a circle for the warm-up." A hand went up in the air. "Everyone quiet down so we can hear Kelsey."

"Can't we skip the warm-up? We only have a few weeks left. We're never going to get it done. We shouldn't waste more time on warm-ups." The class erupted again, several students agreeing vigorously with Kelsey. I held up my hand to get their attention.

"I know many of you are worried that we don't have a script yet and there are only 4 weeks, 3 ½ actually, before the performance. And I know that some of you are frustrated with the warm-ups and games we've been doing. But we actually have made a lot of progress and we have been building the play. You're right that we need to begin writing. By the end of this week, we will have our script. Once we have the script, we can begin actual production: casting, writing the music, building the set, rehearsing scenes."

"But we'll only have 2½ weeks to do all that!" moaned Emma. "We'll never get it all done."

"If you use your time well, you will," I replied. "Two and a half weeks is plenty of time to pull this play together. You don't realize yet just how much work you have already done."

"Yeah, but will it be any good?" muttered Jon. "It probably won't be as good as last year's play."

"That's up to you all," I answered. "I can't guarantee that it will be as good as last year's play. What I can tell you is that you have all the pieces here to make a great play. The tools, the materials are there. What you build now depends on how hard you are willing to work and how ready you are to work together. I think there is potential for something great to come out of this class. But you all have to decide if you are ready to work for it. The hard part is just beginning. Now let's get in a circle."

Warm-ups began with the clapping game to call all the kids into the circle and to focus their attention and ended with a different kind of focus game. After the stretches and "lion roars" and "lemon faces," I would quietly begin by counting "one." Anyone in the circle could say "two," but if two or more people spoke at the same time, we had to begin all over again. The first time we tried the game, we made it up to "three." The exercise requires participants to be tuned in to each other, on the same wavelength. There is no way of knowing who is going to say the next number (going around the circle or developing any kind of pattern is not allowed); the participants have to *feel* it. Today, after several attempts, we made it up to "11." I was feeling hopeful.

Each table group (of four students) started working on a scene from the outline. A few scenes were more fully developed than others because they had grown out of improvisations and critique sessions. Other scenes, especially the tableaus, had been talked about but not yet developed. A couple of the scenes I had drawn from kids' writing about exclusion. The class knew the stories but had not yet tried to drama-tize the scenes. With the more advanced scenes, students began writing a script. But with regard to the less developed scenes, we encouraged groups to play around with ideas first, to try improvising and experi-menting before committing anything to writing.

I wish I could report that all the groups threw themselves into their task, were totally, magically focused, cooperative, and productive. In truth, some groups did. But some groups didn't. One group was work-ing on Scene 6, a tableau about slavery or racism. They were annoyed with me for giving them such a "little" scene. They had wanted to write dialogue for a "real" scene. I explained that every scene was important, as each one built a part of the whole picture. The scene they had to figure out was one of the more difficult ones because it was the least defined. Nevertheless, it was critical because it anchored the historical time line. They had a structure within which to work, using a narrator and a "moving tableau," but they had a lot of leeway to explore different ideas. Figuring that my little lecture had gotten them back on track, I left them to go work with another group.

When I returned to check in on the group about 20 minutes later, I found them degenerating into silliness. "Wanna see what we've come up with?" they asked gleefully. Warily, I agreed. Markie launched into an imitation of a TV news reporter. She described the brutality of slavery in a cheerful, cutesy voice as Randall and Sam acted as slave and master. Two other students sat by bemused, with an expression of "don't blame me, this wasn't my idea" on their faces. I was dismayed. How could they make fun of something so painful? Why weren't they taking this seriously? At first, I didn't know what to say. I wanted to blast them to get serious. But I also did not want this to be *my* show. It had to also be their show. I decided to just be honest.

"I think you're missing the point of this," I said.

"What do you mean?" Markie responded glibly. "You don't like our idea?"

"Not really," I said. "I know that we talked about our play having humor in it and I think humor is really important, but do you really think this is the right place for it?"

"No," said Randall. The others shook their heads, and the façade of silliness caved in. Frustration emerged in its stead.

"But we can't think of anything," whined Markie.

"This is too hard," whined Randall.

"We can't agree on anything," whined Sam.

"You're right; this is hard," I agreed. "Maybe it would help if we talked a little bit about what you are trying to show with this tableau. What do you want the audience to think about?"

"Well, we want to do something about slavery."

"Yeah, but we also want to show that racism is still around."

"It's like the names have changed. People don't call Black people 'savages' anymore, but they still call them names." The group started trying out different possibilities.

"Sounds like you have some good ideas. Keep working on it, try not to get frustrated," I said. "I've got to check in on some other groups. I'll be back."

The next time I checked back with this group, they still didn't have a plan. But they were focused and serious, and they had some ideas. Toward the end of the period, Markie came running over to get me.

"Kathy, Kathy, come hear about our scene," she said excitedly. "It's really good. It's not totally worked out yet, but tell us if you like our idea. See, first the narrator is going to say something about the slave ships coming or something. We still have to work that part out. But then . . ." As she explained to me their plan, the rest of the group waited expectantly.

"Wow!" I exclaimed. "What a fabulous idea! You guys were all whiny and 'we can't do this.' Now you have a great idea. Let's try it out for the class."

Everyone gathered on the rug to see the tableau. On our "stage," Randall, a light-skinned African American boy, stood with his fists clenched opposite Sam, a White boy. Sam had his hand raised as if holding a whip. Markie stood off to the side. She explained to the class, "We haven't written this part yet, but the narrator is going to say something like, 'In 16-something, the first slave ships came bringing millions of Africans to be slaves in the New World.'" Then she pounded her hand on a nearby desk. With each beat, she shouted out a different word. Each word was echoed with a stroke of Sam's imaginary whip, and Randall shrank down, cowering, growing smaller and smaller with each beat.

"Savage!"

"Heathen!"

"Nigger!"

"Lazy!"

"Stupid!"

"Dirty!"

"Animal!"

"Gangster!"

"Criminal!"

With the final word, Randall was crouched on the ground. Sam stood triumphant over him, and snickered. "Their pain echoes through history," Markie stated quietly.

The audience sat for a moment, stunned into silence, and then erupted in applause. The group stood awkwardly in front of their audience, both pleased with themselves and a bit embarrassed. It was time to go, there was no time for feedback, but I grabbed Markie as she started gathering up her books. "I hope you learned something today," I said, a big smile on my face.

"I did," she responded with a laugh.

"What? What did you learn?" I persisted.

"That you don't have to give up on hard things. We thought we couldn't do it, but we pushed through that and came up with something people really liked."

"Yeah," I said. "Don't ever forget that."

She smiled and bounced out of the room.

CHAPTER 12

A Script Emerges

THROUGH THE PROCESS of improvising, writing, critiquing, and revising, the class developed a script with 12 scenes by the end of the week. Unlike a traditional, straightforward narrative, the play unfolded through the interweaving of three different thematic strands. The first strand focused on the parable of the geese. Drawing from our flocking exercise and our warm-ups, a small group of students created a visual image of geese flying together in a V. The play opened with this image, and it reappeared at various interludes throughout the script. The second strand, the historical time line, had three key events illustrated through "moving tableaus": the arrival of Irish immigrants in 1850, 200 years of African slavery, and the 1963 March on Washington. The third strand provided the narrative thread. Each of the scenes in this part of the play grew out of students' actual experiences, activities, or discussions we had had in class.

Scene 1: Sound of wind begins softly and builds. Lights come up on kids in V formation crouched down and curled up. Slowly they begin to rise together until they are fully standing and moving, flocking, following the leader. From off stage a voice yells, "Get those dirty foreigners out of here." There are three sharp raps on a drum. One of the "geese" falls and the rest of the "flock" goes off kilter. Lights and sound of wind fade.

Scene 2: Narrator's voice describes how when Irish first arrived in Boston, they were not welcomed. They were discriminated against, kept out of jobs and housing (No Irish Need Apply), and were generally scorned by native Americans. Students act out tableau of immigrant woman, clutching shawl around her, being turned away by two "Yankee" shopkeepers.

Photo #4: Rodney and Kelsey practice "flocking"
for the opening scene of the play.

Scene 3: In a classroom. Students are gathering for a class. As people
are coming in and taking their seats, a group of kids are talking about
a party that is going to take place that weekend. They chat about who
is going to be invited and who isn't. A Haitian girl, Marie, comes up to
the group, clearly wanting to be invited, but Kate, a White American
girl, rudely excludes her. Monique, a Haitian American girl, starts to
object, but doesn't. Other kids snicker after Marie leaves them.

The teacher comes in and the class begins. The teacher begins to
talk about the last lesson they had on discrimination against the Irish
but explains that today they are going to talk about the New York City
draft riots of 1863. Kids don't understand how Irish could turn around
and discriminate against Blacks. Class enters a discussion about that
and issues around racism. Teacher calls on Marie, who has been very
quiet. Whole class gets very silent and looks at her, waiting. Some kids

are smirking, rolling eyes. She struggles to speak. Teacher doesn't understand her because of her accent. Kids giggle.

Bell rings, and as kids are leaving class, we see Kurt and Rachel talking. They are clearly friends. They make a plan to get together after school to study for a test the next day. Then they run into another group of kids who talk about last night's basketball game. Rachel really wants these kids to like her and accept her into their group. Kurt is left out of conversation. The group invites Rachel to come over and watch the last half of the game on video. She feels conflicted, but she leaves Kurt standing alone.

Scene 4: V formation again. Wind sounds. A narrator tells the first part of the parable of the geese, how geese increase their flying capacity by 71% by flying in the V. Then another voice offstage yells out, "Those people are taking all our jobs!", drum raps three times, and another "goose" goes down. Lights and sound fade.

Scene 5: Two other students from the classroom scene, Pauline, who is White, and Damon, who is Black, are talking about the class at the park. Pauline says she is glad that people aren't racist anymore. Damon says he doesn't agree. People are still prejudiced. It is just more subtle. Three other Black kids come by to play basketball. Damon knows them and says hi. They invite him to play. Pauline asks to play too. They look her over and then say they don't need any more players. Damon joins his friends, still urging Pauline to come along. Pauline says she has to go to store for her mother anyway.

Scene 6: Slavery tableau: (This is the scene Markie's group developed.)

Scene 7: Pauline has left the park and enters a music store. Owner greets her in friendly manner. Another White girl enters store and is also greeted nicely. As they browse, two Black boys come in. Store owner starts following them around. Pauline sees the White girl steal a CD and leave. Owner then notices CD missing and blames Black kids. There is a confrontation between owner and Black kids. Pauline tries to tell owner the truth, but he is too busy screaming at the boys. Black kids walk out angrily as owner goes to call police. Pauline stops him and tells owner it was the girl.

Photo #5: A tense moment in the play as "Kadijah" makes it clear that "Pauline" is not welcome to join in the basketball game.

Scene 8: Instead of the V formation, we see two geese who do a ballet together as narrator tells more of parable of geese. This part tells about how when a goose is sick or injured, another goose will leave the formation to help.

Scene 9: Kate and Monique (from Scene 3) are walking home from school. Monique needs to stop in a store to buy some things for home. It is a Haitian store. Kate is clearly uncomfortable and questions Monique about various unfamiliar items (plantains and sugar cane). She is even more uncomfortable when Monique converses in Creole with store owners. She wonders aloud why these people don't learn English. Monique leaves her in exasperation.

Scene 10: Kate arrives home and plops down in a chair. After several unsuccessful attempts to call friends, she gets out her history book and falls asleep as she tries to study. Lights dim to half and several people dressed in bright colors, one in all blue, another all purple, another all red, emerge, babbling in a strange language (based on BAFA BAFA game). Kate gets up and wanders through them, confused and frightened by the strange culture. The characters begin shouting at her and then suddenly disappear, leaving Marie, the Haitian girl. She walks silently toward Kate, looks at her intently, and then disappears. Kate returns to her chair and "wakes up" from her dream, clearly shaken.

Scene 11: Time-line narrator announces the March on Washington in 1963 when people of all races and backgrounds came together for equality and justice for all. As we hear Martin Luther King's speech, one by one, students walk on stage and sit down in a V formation with backs to audience as if they are at the rally listening to the speaker.

Scene 12: As King's voice fades, a voice offstage calls out a line from students' "I Am What I Am" poems focusing on their ethnic diversity. With each line, one of the "marchers" stands up and begins flocking. Soon all marchers are standing and flocking in the V formation. The scene ends with marchers breaking into a hip-hop dance as the rest of the cast gradually joins them on stage.

Although the script was not totally finished, we knew who our characters were and where each scene took place. Now we needed a title. We began brainstorming a list: *Lessons From Geese, Geese, What We Learned, Exclusion, Flying in a V.* There were lots of other suggestions, but nothing seemed quite right. I asked students to think about it overnight so we could take a vote the next day.

The next morning, I noticed a few more suggestions had been added to the list. As I read through them, one stood out—*Why Fly That Way?* I still don't know who made the suggestion (no one claimed responsibility), but that day the class overwhelmingly approved it as our official title.

So we had a script. We had a title. We were now ready to begin production. We formed five different committees: assistant directors (I had learned the hard way that *I* needed to be the executive director), set design and construction, costumes, publicity, and music. Students signed up to be on the committee that interested them most. June was in charge of the set design crew. They examined our performance space (the school cafeteria), reviewed each scene for prop needs, sketched possible sets, and started to build and paint. Jackie supervised the costume and publicity committees. The costume committee made a list of all the characters, what each should wear, and started soliciting donations of clothes. The publicity committee's main charge was to design a poster to advertise the play. They came up with several creative designs and then chose a final one.

I met with the assistant directors to cast the play. Casting has always been done democratically in my classroom. Also, I have always insisted on a policy that everyone act. Students can request a large or a small part, but I want everyone to have the experience of performing at least one line on stage. For some students, that one line has been a tremendous challenge. It has pushed them to experiment in a new arena. Each year, at least a couple of students discover, much to their surprise, that they enjoy being on stage. "I wish I had had the courage to go for a bigger part," wrote one girl. "Next time I will know I can do it and I won't be so afraid."

The assistant directors made a list of all the characters in the play and asked each student to rank the parts he or she was interested in playing. We then made a grid with every character on one axis and every member of the class on the other, and we filled in the chart according to each student's request. The assistant directors worked as a group to cast the parts. I instructed them to use two guidelines in their casting decisions. First, they should think about who could play which part best. We did not audition for roles. Because we had been doing improvs and roleplays and because the students had created and experimented with the characters, the assistant directors had a good sense of each student's talents. Second, they should try to honor people's requests for particular parts. If someone indicated wanting a large role, but the part requested first had been given to someone else, the assistant directors would try to find another comparable part. Ultimately, though, final decisions were made in the best interest of the play as a whole.

I maintained the right of final veto or ultimate decision-making, but I never used it. In our first play, *On the Line* (Korty, 1979), the students cast a Haitian girl who had just been mainstreamed into an English-speaking classroom in a major role. Although they had rarely heard her speak, they thought her personality fit the character. They also cast a boy with a serious speech disability as a union organizer who had a one-and-a-half-page monologue. In each case, they recognized the risks but felt that with support and practice, Jodelle and Chris would be great in the parts. They were right. Jodelle never dropped a line, and Chris delivered his speech from a soap box without falter. Later, when asked how he felt about doing the play, Chris wrote, "I felt like a knight in shining armor and I could do anything!" I was convinced that our process worked.

This year, as the assistant directors reviewed students' requests, we realized we had an unusual issue to resolve. Manuela, an African American girl, had requested the part of Pauline. In past years, we had always cast parts regardless of people's race or background. In *On the Line*, Jodelle had played a French Canadian mother. Lori, also a Haitian girl, had played a Jewish child in another play. Emily, who was White, had played her younger sister. We tended not to cast across gender lines, but race had never been a factor. We all liked it that way.

In our play this year, however, race was a critical factor. Much of the play focused on racial and cultural differences. Pauline is a White girl who has a discussion with Damon, an African American boy, about racism. From her perspective, racism is a thing of the past. She says, "I've lived here all my life and I've never seen anything racist happen." Damon responds, "That's because you're White. It doesn't happen to you. You don't see it because it never happens to you."

The directors were concerned. "It's not really going to make sense if Manuela plays Pauline," said Sam. "At one point, Damon says, 'Look at my skin and look at yours.' Manuela is darker than Imani [who was playing Damon]. Won't that be confusing?"

"Yeah, but Pauline is a big part, and Manuela really wants a big part. There aren't any other good ones left. Plus Manuela is a really good actress. We need to use her well," responded Sarah. "It feels really weird to be making decisions on the basis of someone's skin color."

"Yeah, last year's play was all mixed. People's skin color didn't matter," piped in Randall.

"But this is different," said Sam. "This play is about racism and people judging each other. It is going to be really confusing to the audience if Black kids are playing White kids and vice versa."

"Yeah, I guess you're right," conceded Sarah. "We should give Nicole Pauline's role and try and figure out a good part for Manuela. She'd be a great Kadijah. Maybe she can do a big chunk in the last scene too [which hadn't yet been written]."

"I think you guys are right," I said. "Someone should talk with Manuela and explain. She'll understand."

Manuela didn't understand. She was furious. "I can't believe this," she fumed. "Here we are writing a play about exclusion and *I'm* being excluded because I'm not the right color? That's not fair!" Although she was not interested in her classmates' explanations, she grudgingly accepted the role of Kadijah. I had thought that she would eventually get over her disappointment about not getting the part she wanted, but rehearsals were tense as her anger bubbled just below the surface. In fact, the tension was starting to spread to other students, endangering the fragile sense of community that had begun to build. Something had to be done to stem the rising tide of resentment. I asked Manuela to meet with me privately.

"Manuela, I know you're upset about not getting the part of Pauline," I started, "but it's getting in the way of making the play work as a whole."

"I know," she responded. "I know I have to let go of this, but it is so hard. I understand why they cast Nicole in the part. Really, I do. But it felt so bad to have somebody make a decision based on my color and not on how good a job I would do. I understand it all, but it still feels really bad. That's what we've been talking about all year, how people excluded others because they were Chinese or Irish. I didn't think it would happen in my own classroom."

I felt terrible. I had thought Manuela was just being a sore sport about not getting the part she wanted. But this wasn't just about disappointment. It was about how deep the issues of racism and exclusion are in our society. I realized how, inadvertently, we had touched a deep wound. All year we had explored how community breaks down and what makes communities strong. One thing we had learned was the importance of listening to each other. In fact, the scene with Pauline and Damon was about learning to listen to and validate other people's experiences, especially when they differed from one's own. Now Manuela was challenging me to practice what I had been preaching. I shared these thoughts with her. She began to relax and we talked for a long time.

"So, what do you think we should do about this?" I asked finally.

"Well . . . ," she began slowly, "I don't think we should change the parts. It probably is better to have Nicole play Pauline and I actually like playing Kadijah. It would be great, though, if there is another part for me in the last scene. But if it doesn't work out, that's okay. Mostly I just wanted you to understand how I felt."

I felt chastened by this incident. Like Pauline in the play, I hadn't understood, or had at least underestimated, the pain created by this casting dilemma because I was White. I had never lost access to something I wanted badly because of my color. Furthermore, it reminded me of the importance of not making assumptions about other people's feelings. If I had just pushed Manuela to "get over it," I would have lost a valuable learning opportunity and silenced her. Our rehearsals also would have erupted. While it was a painful experience (especially for Manuela), we all learned something from it (I especially), and I was pleased that we were able to get back on track working together.

But, just when I was growing hopeful about how much the class was finally coming together, Emma asked to meet with me. Emma had also not gotten a part she had wanted badly. I was prepared to give her a pep talk about her role. She came in during recess and started haltingly, "I wasn't sure I should tell you about this, but then I thought about how we've talked all year about community and supporting each other and how people step on other people, and I thought you would probably want to know."

She paused, and I waited for her to continue, wondering what was coming next. "You know that I wanted the part of Kate and Anna got it instead of me? I was disappointed, of course, but I understood. Anna will do a really good job, probably better than I would, and that's what's most important. But yesterday at recess, Kelsey and Christian [two of the assistant directors] came up to me and said that they were glad I didn't get the part and that they never even really considered me . . ." Her voice trailed off and she bit her lip. I waited, dismayed by this report. She went on. "Well, I think that was kind of crummy. I mean, why did they say that? I thought we were supposed to be building trust in each other, but that doesn't make me feel very trusting."

I was shocked. Things had been going well. The Pauline crisis had been resolved. I had been so pleased with the way the kids were pulling for each other. We talked a lot about how we were finally flying in the V, and we had all felt the power of our collective work. Or at least I thought we had. I didn't understand why Kelsey and Christian would do that to Emma.

"Emma, I am so sorry this happened to you," I said. "It is very upsetting, but I am really glad you told me about it. What they did is not okay, and I promise you I will follow up on this."

Later that day, I found Kelsey and Christian and told them I needed to see them the next day at recess. Emma also came, and I started by relating to the other two what Emma had told me the day before. "That's

Emma's side of the story," I said. "Do either of you have a different version?" They looked down at the desks sheepishly.

"I don't know why we did it," Kelsey said. "I know it was wrong." Christian nodded in agreement. "We're sorry, Emma."

I sat for a few moments and then said, "What you two did is very, very serious. You are both assistant directors for the play. To be an effective director, you have to have the trust and respect of the actors you are working with. You just blew that. I don't know how you expect Emma to work with you now, or anybody else, for that matter. I'm thinking of firing you both. It's too bad, though, because we could use you. You have the potential to be good directors. Or you can find a way to make this up to Emma that rebuilds some trust. Saying sorry here isn't enough. I'm not going to tell you what to do; you need to think about that for yourselves and work it out with Emma. I'll leave the choice up to you." All three students nodded solemnly. "If you decide to stay on, you can't make a mistake like this again. Don't tell me now; I want you to think about it. Let me know tomorrow what your decision is."

Wasn't this ever going to get easier? Weren't we ever going to reach a place where we could count on each other? Every time I felt we were getting close, something like this seemed to happen. But then I stepped back from the moment and realized that we had indeed been getting closer. So often, I expect the journey to be a smooth and simple one. But real growth and learning is rarely linear and direct. We move a few steps forward, take a couple to the side, sometimes move backward, often go in circles, but when we keep working toward our goal, we do make progress.

The next day, Kelsey and Christian reported to me that they had made up with Emma. They apologized to me, too, and promised earnestly to be supportive of their colleagues. When I checked in with Emma, she was happy and felt the incident was resolved. I thought about the lessons learned. Maybe this whole incident wasn't so terrible after all. Emma learned to speak up for herself and to defend her right to be treated with respect. Christian and Kelsey learned to take responsibility for hurting another person's feelings. I learned that kids can and do make mistakes but, when given an opportunity, they can learn from them.

CHAPTER 13

Adding Music

A NEW ELEMENT in our play this year was the addition of original music. Newell Hendricks is a composer who has worked with young people of all ages writing their own songs. I first met Newell a few years earlier when our daughters had had the same teacher. That year, he helped the students write a musical revue about their class. It was marvelous. The songs were wonderfully creative and the children performed with zest and pride. I asked Newell then if he would want to venture into music-making in the more turbulent waters of middle school. He was definitely interested, and for years we tossed around the idea of collaborating on a play. This year, with his daughter Anna in the class, the time seemed finally right.

I was a bit apprehensive, though. Could Newell engage these seventh and eighth graders in writing songs? Would they open up to an outsider, to a parent? Third graders don't worry about looking cool. The inhibitions of adolescence haven't set in yet. I thought my students would balk at adding music. I worried that they would resist it as corny. It was hard enough getting some students to stand up on stage and speak. How could we get them to stand up and sing?

Newell began visiting the class regularly when we first started developing the basic concepts of the play after April vacation. He participated in our warm-ups and listened carefully as students talked about the kind of play they wanted to make. When he broached the subject of creating music for the play, several students were very enthusiastic. We discovered that quite a number of them played instruments: piano, drums, flute, guitar, violin, and clarinet. We had a veritable orchestra. We also had a group of strong singers. Newell assured me that he could find a way to include them all.

His first step was to meet with a group of interested students to review the play. They looked for possible spots to insert a song or an instrumental bridge and then presented their suggestions to the whole class. Once we had general agreement on this, small groups of students met to work on lyrics. These groups generated text in a variety of ways. Willy and Caitlin worked on a song for the "Irish tableau," in which a young Irish immigrant is turned away and scorned by two storekeepers. Newell asked them to think about phrases they associated with this scene. They came up with:

"'No Irish need apply,' say the signs and the prejudiced employers."
"I can only work in factories for pennies."
"I am Irish, hate and exclusion fill the streets."
"My children have no childhood."
"Everyone must work or die."

Next, he asked them to pick one of these phrases and repeat it, trying to find within it its natural rhythm. Then he asked them to sing the line— whatever came to mind, whatever came out. Whereas Caitlin welcomed the opportunity to sing (she had a lovely lyrical voice), Willy adamantly refused. That was going too far for him. But he encouraged Caitlin, praised her singing, offered his opinion on different melodic lines, and helped to shape the piece. Before long, they had a simple but haunting song:

I can only work in factories for pennies.
My children have no childhood,
Everyone must work or die.
I am Irish,
No Irish need apply.

Newell later added a baseline and parts for violin, flute, keyboard, and guitar. The song was used not only in the tableau but instrumentally in other parts of the play as well.

Another group used a different approach to develop lyrics. Regine, Mendette, and Meribah remembered a poem we had read aloud in class earlier in the year during our immigration unit. "You've got to live in somebody else's country to understand" was written by Noy Chou, a Cambodian student at a nearby high school.

What is it like to be an outsider?
    What is it like to sit in the class where everyone has blond hair and you have black hair?

What is it like when the teacher says, "Whoever wasn't born here raise your hand."
And you are the only one.
Then, when you raise your hand, everybody looks at you and makes fun of you.
You have to live in somebody else's country to understand. (as cited in *Facing History and Ourselves*, 1994, p. 31)

The poem captured the pain of being a newcomer, and the girls, two of whom were Haitian, were determined to bring its message into the play. They started by highlighting lines that they especially liked and then wrote some of their own words. Gradually a shape and a rhythm began to emerge.

Do you know what it's like to be different?
Do you know what it's like to be me?
To be excluded,
To be secluded
In somebody else's country?

Do you know what it's like to be labeled?
Do you know what it's like to be me?
To be called dumb
Or to be called a "just-come"
In somebody else's country?

They struggled with different tunes and couldn't settle on one that seemed to create the right mood. Finally, Anna was invited to give it a try. An experienced musician, she eventually came up with a melody that pleased everyone. The song was sung by two Haitian girls during the dream sequence.

Emma wanted to write a song following the scene where Pauline witnesses two young Black men being falsely accused of shoplifting. She had a vision of the White girl, the Black teenager, and the storekeeper singing their own perspective of the scene. She struggled with the lyrics for a while, critiqued her work several times with other students, and finally settled on a duet. Pauline's lines were:

Something I've never seen before with my own eyes,
A couple of Black kids were accused, much to my surprise,

Accused of stealing something that they didn't even touch,
Is it that we look at skin color too much?

Nicole, who was playing the part of Pauline, had a clear soprano voice and a marvelous innocence about her when she sang. She was thrilled to have a song. But when Newell approached Chris, who played the part of the accused teenager, he refused to sing. Chris had a fine tenor voice and was active in his church choir, but he was not going to sing in this scene. As he looked at the lines, though, he started speaking, and then rapping, them. "I can do it this way," he suggested. The next day he brought in a tape with a heavy backbeat to accompany the rap.

Something just happened that made me mad,
I didn't take a thing, I think I've just been had.
If the owner hadn't followed us around his store,
He would've caught the thief instead of chasing us out the door.

In the play, this song comes at the end of the shoplifting scene. The lights dim and Nicole, with guitar accompaniment, sings her verse to the audience. Then Chris steps out of the shadows rapping hard to a driving beat. They then turn to each other, alternating lines—Nicole's questioning melody and Chris's angry rap. The effect is powerful.

Like the songwriters, the instrumentalists rallied to the task. Case was one of our flutists. All year, Case had been painfully shy in class. She did not like to speak in front of any group and was even reluctant to read aloud although she was a very strong reader. She worked hard at being invisible. But when the opportunity came to play her flute, she was eager. She was not a sophisticated musician, but she worked hard to learn a simple harmony for the Irish song and practiced regularly at home. She was willing to rehearse at any time. She would give up recess, lunch, or stay after school. One day I watched her as some students experimented with using the piece as accompaniment to a ballet Meribah and Anna had choreographed. She stood tall and played the melody with confidence. I realized that Case wasn't trying to be invisible anymore.

All in all, 12 students contributed to creating four songs for the play, 14 played an instrument, and five sang during the performance. The process had been so collaborative I hadn't realized just how many people had been involved until I spoke with Newell after the play. Once again, I recognized that my own fears, inhibitions, and assumptions had nearly prevented a marvelous opportunity for many students to grow. I had been worried that no one would want to participate musically. But for some students, the music had become their special domain, their unique contribution, their way to shine. As I looked back on our discussion at the beginning of the year about multiple intelligences, I realized that I should not have been surprised by students' responsiveness.

Some of our musicians were remarkably talented, but others were not. Newell, however, had a gift for making both music and the making of music accessible to anyone who wanted to try it out. The songs seemed to come from within the students. They were built from the themes and issues that young people cared about. He drew on their skills and strengths and stretched them just enough so that they surprised themselves with what they could do. By showing them the natural rhythm in language and the power of a simple melodic line, Newell helped students discover that making music did not have to be something *other* people did.

As opening night drew nearer, lines between our committees began to blur. If a job needed to be done, whoever was available did it. With rehearsals, songwriting, and set construction all happening at the same time, logistics began to get very complicated. We often interrupted the songwriters or the set builders to pull them into a scene rehearsal. Sometimes, if a musician was working with Newell, we would have to juggle our rehearsal schedule. At times I wondered about the wisdom of having all students engaged in so many different aspects of production.

But the craziness of logistics was worth it to me. Along with craziness came ownership. The students "owned" this play. They had conceived it, planned it, and built it step by step. It was a public forum for their thoughts and beliefs. Along with ownership came commitment. They wanted to be heard and they wanted to be taken seriously. Because this play represented them, students were invested in doing their highest caliber work. They knew that the higher the quality of their work, the more powerful its impact would be on their audience.

Along with this commitment to building a piece of top-notch theater came the urgency of community. Students realized that they needed each other. If the actors didn't know their lines, it would hurt their play. If the set designers did a sloppy job, it would hurt their play. If the props weren't in the right place, it would hurt their play. To make the best possible play, students knew that everyone had to put in his or her best effort. They finally understood that working together as a caring community made our product stronger.

I wanted to kick myself. All year long, I had been pushing kids to work together, to establish trust among themselves, to be willing to take risks, to follow through on responsibilities to others, to support and encourage their peers rather than tease and "dis" each other. I believed that I had to see evidence of this before we could begin the play. I had seen glimpses of growth during the year: the Expert Projects, the ice skating trip, some class discussions. But it was the playmaking process itself that forged a profound commitment to the community. The play called for a deep understanding of history, personal reflection, and an examination of one's own values and actions. It demanded that students take risks, try new things, and trust each other. Its success depended on each one's taking responsibility, caring for each other, and giving each other critical but supportive feedback. It inspired them to do their best and to demand the best of each other. Perhaps this would never have happened without all the groundwork we laid over the year. But that May, I vowed that if I ever did another play with seventh and eighth graders, I would start working on it from the first day of school.

CHAPTER 14

The Performance

I think that we have a good play, but we need to work together on getting everything set up and say the lines louder. I feel really comfortable with my scene in the play . . . but I am really worried about my last line. . . . I feel that I am going to forget my line. I am also worried about losing the things I brought in. The dance scene is the scene I am really uncomfortable with because I feel that people are just going to mess up. I am proud of this play and I think it will be a big success. (Regine)

I can't believe we have four more days before it happens. The time really flew by, and even though at times it seems hopeless, I know we are going to make it. Tuesday was a very bad day. We were asked to move from three different practice locations and by the time we started rehearsing everyone was off focus, and we never really got back on track. . . . It was very frustrating, we got much less done than we should have. (Sarah)

Today was great. I got my lines down, and I know how the scenes go. We will have to readjust our timing when we do it in the cafeteria [our stage area] but we are doing good. . . . I think I should practice how I stand, and to look more confident, maybe in front of a mirror. (Willy)

I don't really know what to think about the play at this point . . . I guess I will feel better when we have the total dress rehearsal on Wednesday, but I don't know. We really only have TWO more full days to practice and then we're on. . . . If we pull this off it will be amazing. This isn't to say I don't think we're gonna pull it off . . . I don't want our play to be mediocre. I want this play to really have an impact . . . Kathy, a question for U. Do U think we can pull it off and make an impact? (Markie)

I have always been confident about the play since it was first mentioned. I never had a doubt about it, never was nervous or thought I was going to mess up . . . until now. When I think of it, I get scared and have butterflies in my stomach. I just want to scream it all out. The nervousness and the excitement. I really don't want to mess up because I don't want to let my classmates down. And I don't want to let you down. So I'm going to try my best. WISH ME LUCK!!! (Prakan)

A S OPENING NIGHT GREW CLOSER, excitement gripped the class with one hand and anxiety with the other. Students asked to stay in at recess to rehearse a scene just one more time; others stayed after school to paint the finishing touches on the scenery. Meribah and Anna worked on the timing of their ballet with the musicians and narrator. Regine, Mendette, and Markie hustled to choreograph a hip-hop dance for our finale that everyone could do. When I stopped Imani in the hall for a 10-second diction lesson, he smiled and promised he would rehearse at home.

The play today was much better than I thought it would be. Yesterday, I didn't see the whole run through, but from what I saw, it looked like we needed a lot of work. Today, I am happy to say that almost all of Kathy's humanities kids do very well when they are under pressure. There are some things everybody needs to work on, including me. Here is my list:
Scene 1: Sing loudly, don't be afraid.
Scene 5: Speak loudly, leave quickly.
Scene 5: Be on cue, drum loudly.
(Manuela)

If one more person tells me I need to speak louder . . . I'll explode. I guess what I mean to say is that at least five people told me to talk louder, and only one said, "nice work." Tonight I'm gonna practice my volume (raising it). Also, tomorrow I'll move more props. (Seth)

People really need to be completely off stage when another scene that they are not in is going on. . . . I hope we make the transitions from scenes better. . . . In general, most people need to work on projecting, but I really want to work on slowing down my lines. (Markie)

Something wonderful was happening. For so much of the year, I had urged, prodded, demanded higher standards from students. But as the performance drew closer and closer, students were setting their own goals, holding themselves to high expectations. They no longer needed me as an engine to drive and motivate them. We were finally flying in the V.

> June 1: Today we had our dress rehearsal with an audience. I can't believe how well this went. Kids' energy was really up. They sounded great and looked great. I think back to a few weeks ago and I am amazed. These guys have really come a long way.

The jitters were palpable on opening night. I was nervous, too. How strong was our community? Could it withstand the pressure of performance? Would the kids be able to maintain their focus and sense of purpose? What would happen if someone made a mistake? Could we continue to fly in the V? Would they respond as professionals or would they turn on each other in panic? I knew, in a way I had not known before, that these young people could hold each other up. They were certainly capable of it; they just had to make the choice.

The cast began arriving an hour before show time. With them, they brought bad news. Catherine, who played the teacher, a significant part in Scene 4, was terribly sick with strep throat and had a temperature of 104°. There was no way she would be able to go on stage. Before their alarm was able to spread, however, Sarah volunteered to fill in for her. She got a copy of the script and scurried off with a few of the actors from that scene to study her lines. "That's sort of like the geese," commented Manuela. I looked at her quizzically. "You know," she said, "when one goose is sick or wounded? The others go to help her out, right?" I smiled. I didn't need to worry about this crew. They would be there for each other; they were already there.

The audience started arriving early. Cast members nervously milled about our makeshift stage (in the cafeteria because our school has no auditorium) until we called them together in the nearby music room for the preshow pep talk. It was not easy focusing 38 anxious young adolescents, but we managed to get their attention, go through a few calming warm-up exercises, review a couple of rocky transitions, and remind them about diction and projection. I congratulated them on their outstanding work. Above all, I urged them, remember to fly in the V. If

Photo #6: A few students worked together to design
the play's poster and program.

someone drops a line, misses a beat, forgets a cue, or freezes up, it will be okay if everyone is in the V.

After a few moments of silence to collect our thoughts, the room erupted in exuberant energy and the cast flowed out, ready to take their positions. A few students picked their way through the dark onto the "stage" where, in a V formation, they crouched down, hugging their knees. The rest of the cast assumed their stations behind the audience. I took my customary seat, front row, stage right. The cafeteria was pitch-black and silent. The audience waited in anticipation. Slowly, almost inaudible at first, a sound, created by a melange of voices and instruments, began to fill the space. The lights came up slowly on the stage; the sound of the wind built into an open-throated chant. The bodies on stage began to unfold into slow, graceful, unified flight. The show had begun.

Sarah did a wonderful stand-in job as the teacher that night, and in spite of a few misplaced props and a few missed cues, our first performance was a huge success. I was thrilled and so were the kids. But the tough part was yet to come. Our first performance had been to a fairly sympathetic audience of parents and friends. The greatest challenge for these students would be to perform for their peers. The feelings of self-consciousness that we had worked hard to overcome began to creep in again. Students worried, Am I going to look stupid? Are my friends going to tease me? Are people going to think that I am really the character I am just playing? They also worried about the tradition of theater they were upholding. Will people like our play? Will they think it is as good as last year's play? Furthermore, this play, more than any other my classes had done, directly addressed some tense and difficult issues in the school. How will students respond? Will they feel threatened or challenged? Will they just dismiss us? Or will they take our thoughts and our work seriously?

As we prepared for our school performance, I assured the cast that they were ready. "There may be a few people in the audience who give you a hard time. Sometimes kids will yell out something or act silly because they are jealous. They wish they could be doing what you are doing. Don't pay them any mind. Hold on to your professionalism. Remember, if you perform from your heart, there is no way you can fail to win your audience."

The show went well. The audience laughed when they were supposed to laugh, and were absorbed in the drama of the conflicts presented. They burst into enthusiastic applause at the end, and friends rushed up to congratulate cast members. During the day, teachers and students stopped us in the hall to comment on both the professionalism of the performance and the power of the ideas presented in the story. It seemed that our play had provoked a number of class discussions about issues of tolerance and intolerance, inclusion and exclusion, tension and acceptance in our school. One Haitian bilingual class took notes on their reactions to the play and sent them down the hall to us. Their newsprint read:

> Play tried to teach people who are not bilingual how to be with bilingual people. By comparing people and geese in a play, they were able to talk about color and bilingual issues. Still, in our class, almost half the class "felt hurt"—it brought past feelings of hurt having experienced the same thing [as depicted in the play]; it was the reality of the play that hurt; it was difficult for some "to see" their experiences—
>
> We liked many things about the play: in the dream the girl experienced how it feels to be different; at the end people identified their differences, but then came together; the end, in formation, when Mendette said she was proud to be Haitian; liked the parts in Creole; the actors "knew what they were doing," and the reality is these things happen everyday; the singing, the instruments were important and wonderful; great use of all talents of kids.

They finished their message with a poem:

> Geese
> Smart Encouraging
> Helping Flying Supporting
> Flying in a V formation with love
> Together

> from Room 304 to the Graham and Parks 311 Players

My students were pleased that their work had elicited such thoughts and emotions, and I was thrilled. So often in school it seems as if we teachers are the ones asking questions, raising issues, pointing out contradictions, trying to challenge our students to think deeply. How often do students have the experience of challenging each other's thinking?

It is tremendously validating for young people to express their ideas and to be taken seriously by their whole community, including adults and other students.

> June 2: Three shows down, one to go. Yesterday at this time, I felt absolutely dead. The thought of doing three more shows seemed like an insurmountable hurdle. Today I feel sad that we have only one show left. Well, not totally sad, but there is a sadness to lose this great feeling and go back to life as usual.

For our final performance, I told students to arrive at 7:00 P.M., a half hour rather than an hour before show time. There was really no need to come any earlier. Although there had been a few rough spots in the morning performance, we had ironed out most of the glitches during the day. All props and costumes were in place. Chairs were set up. Lights were ready. We were ready. I wanted them to be rested and relaxed when they showed up that night.

I arrived at the school at 6:45 P.M. to find several cast members already there. They were milling about quietly and when they saw me, some rushed up to ask if there was anything that needed to be done. I shook my head, I really couldn't think of anything, and I told them just to stay out of trouble and not wander off.

As I was getting my notes organized and checking on a few last-minute details, someone put in a tape of rap music on the boom box. I was about to chastise somebody for messing around with the equipment when I looked up to an amazing scene. On our "stage" (a 15-by-15-foot square delineated by heavy tar paper covering the institutional checkerboard flooring of the cafeteria), the kids had started dancing together. Unlike typical school dances where students move only under the cover of darkness, the stage lights were on full and about 20 kids were squeezed together, laughing and bouncing to the rhythm of the music. Emma was dancing with Chris who was dancing with Manuela who was dancing with Damien who was dancing with Sarah who was dancing with Prakan. They were all dancing together. As more people arrived, they joined in, creating a giant undulating amoebic creature. June, Jackie, and I watched from the back of the cafeteria, and I thought back to the beginning of the year. This was the same group in which so-and-so refused to sit with so-and-so and so-and-so couldn't stand so-and-so. This crew had come a long way.

As we gathered "backstage" (in the music room that adjoins the cafeteria) for our warm-ups, I began thinking about my usual little pep talk. What could I say? Here it was June 2. The eighth graders had 7 days of school left. They had already performed two shows and done extremely well. I worried that they would get too cocky and overconfident. That's when mistakes get made, and I didn't want them to close on a sloppy show. How was I going to get them to focus and maintain the concentration we had worked so hard to achieve?

Then it hit me. It really didn't matter whether or not they executed the perfect performance. It really didn't matter if the plantains were forgotten again or if Meribah's guitar was slightly out of tune. What mattered was that Clara had searched down the plantains that afternoon and put them in the right place because she didn't want to let Tessa down. What mattered was that Chris and Sarah had worked together during recess to make sure his rap tape was cued up to just the right spot. What mattered was that just minutes earlier they had all been dancing together, feeling good about themselves and about each other. What mattered was that they had finally come together, relied on and trusted each other, to create a powerful piece of drama that gave voice to serious issues that affected their lives, their school, and their community.

We stood in a large circle, 38 young performers, June, Jackie, Newell, and I. I looked around the room at each of their faces. For once they were absolutely quiet, looking at me expectantly. I was a bit surprised by their attentiveness. "I'm not sure what to say to you tonight," I began. "Normally, I would be warning you not to let yourselves get sloppy. You've done two great shows, and the tendency is to let your concentration go. So I guess you should keep that in mind. But as I look around this room, I know we don't need to worry about anything. You know why? Because we have already been victorious. We have already achieved our success. No matter what happens tonight with this show, we have already succeeded. Of course, I want people to think about their lines and remember to speak loudly and not to forget their cues and so on. But, to me, all that is icing on the cake. When I think back to the beginning of this year and think about how far we have come together . . ." I paused, feeling my throat thicken and my eyes begin to get blurry. The room was absolutely silent. I looked at them all as I struggled to hold back my tears. "We have really learned to fly in the V. Together we have created a piece of art, a serious, high-quality piece of art. You have given me the best gift a teacher could ever have. Thank you. Go out there tonight and have fun."

That night they shone. I had been totally pleased with their earlier performances, but those paled in comparison to this final show. Not a line was dropped or a cue missed. But even more, somehow the show seemed fuller. They boldly filled the characters they had created; they sang from their hearts and played their instruments with conviction. I forgot to be the anxious director and, along with the rest of the audience, was caught up in the magic they created. When Marceline sang "I just want to hide away 'cause I'm feelin' lonely," I got chills. When Prakan leaned sadly against his locker as his friend abandoned him for someone more popular, my heart ached. When Peter led a group of geese in flocking, I was mesmerized. And when Mendette proclaimed in the final line of the play, "I am what I am and I am proud. You can tell because every second my heart beats, it pounds," my own heart swelled with pride in them all.

> It went great! Everything was great! People were crying and laughing. It really got [the audience] thinking. Even I cried. Everyone was there for each other and it went even better than the last time. There was a strong community. We flyed [*sic*] together and it showed. This play brought out the best of everyone. I never thought this was possible, but it is. Now I've learned to believe in everything I do. (Rejeanne)

> I felt wonderful about how we did. Sometimes I'd had doubts about whether we could pull it off, but we REALLY did! (Markie)

> We did it! And it was great! It was a pretty new thing for me to do. I had never written and performed a play before. (Willy)

> I have to admit I was kind of not strong about the success of this play, but today's performances proved me wrong. I think the performance we did was great . . . I think people got the message about our play. I think it was even better than last year's play. It was a strong piece. Even though I knew what was next in the play, I still cried. I almost cried when Marceline was singing. I also saw some of my peers wiping their eyes after that scene. Today was a great day. (Regine)

CHAPTER 15

Lessons Learned

THE DAYS AFTER the play glowed. The students basked in their success. They felt good about themselves and good about each other. They recognized what they had achieved. But I wondered, what had they learned? We had focused on the theme of community all year. What had we finally discovered about it through this process of playmaking? When I asked this question in the beginning of the year, students' responses were glib, pat, superficial. "A community is a group of people who live or work together." "We are a community because we share a common space and a common purpose." When I asked it again, a different understanding of community and how it can help us to learn and grow together was evident in their responses.

I learned that a community is like lifting up something together. If one person lets go, the whole thing falls on the rest of them. Whenever one of us was not there for a scene, it made a big difference. The whole work fell down the drain. But, in the end, we were really there for each other.

I started raising my hand and telling my ideas to my peers for once in my life. This play taught me to open up my inner self and spread my ideas.

I learned that if everyone goes all the way they can make it work. I mean, we pulled this thing off in a month. That's community if I ever saw it.

I knew what made community work, but I had never seen it with this class. The play really showed how to make community work. When you experience it, it is a very great feeling. It is when everyone is going all out 101% that we just fly by everybody and things become easy.

I learned a lot about community in this play. I learned we can work together very well in this situation. I also became friends with people I did not know or did not like. I can talk to people now that I don't usually talk to, and you can just really feel the sense of community in the room.

I learned that building a community doesn't just take TOTAL loyalty, companionship, and devotion, but it helps. Community is when we ignore the fact that we don't like or misunderstand someone. That wasn't always displayed: people had complaints, arguments, and annoyances, but we did OK with the whole trust thing.

Sometimes people don't always fly in the V. One thing can break it down. At the beginning of the year, we didn't fly in the V. But as we worked together through the year, we built up the strength that made us fly that way.

And what did I learn? I had been on a mission all year to teach these students something about how they learn, about how to work together to strengthen themselves and the community of which they are a part. But once again, I found myself in the role of the learner.

June 5: Community comes when people share a common goal. We don't have to all be the same. In fact, our work was stronger because of our differences—we needed hip hoppers and ballet dancers, singers and painters, people who love to act and people who want to move scenery.

But community doesn't just happen because we are all in the same space, or reading the same book, or even sharing our writing. Community developed because we depended on each other, we needed each other, and yet when one of us fell out of formation (like Catherine), we were strong enough to hold up the garbage truck without them.

It also developed out of struggle. Our high was so high because our lows were so low. . . . We need to be willing to feel the pain, the fear, the unknown, to be tired, the sweat, to also feel the exaltation of creating something good. Good? It was great!

Letting Go and Risk-taking

What else had I learned? Perhaps my biggest personal challenge had been overcoming my own fears of the unknown and trusting in the creative process. I had spoken to my students all year about the importance of risk-taking in learning, the need to leave their comfort zones and experiment in unknown territory. I firmly believe that this is where real growth and learning take place for all people, both in and out of school. And yet, I realized how reluctant I had been to leave my own comfort zone of lesson plans and curriculum to give students the space to create original, thoughtful work. In *The Having of Wonderful Ideas*, Eleanor Duckworth (1996) describes the importance of creating time in the classroom for students to play, to ponder, to muck about with a subject. Given this opportunity to explore, students become both motivated and invested in their learning. This is where real understanding begins.

As teachers, however, we find it very difficult to let go of the control. We feel in charge when students are sitting quietly at their desks. We feel we are doing our job when we talk and they listen. In fact, for some teachers, maintaining control is the ultimate goal. But that kind of control can be very deceptive. Being in charge doesn't mean that we are teaching. We don't *really* know what is going on in those young heads. I can deliver my interesting and well-planned lecture, students can be sitting quietly at their desks, we can read the chapter in the book, we can "cover" the curriculum. But that does not necessarily mean that the students have learned what we think we have taught them. I discover the real effectiveness of my teaching and the real depth of their learning when I loosen the reins and create space for them to ponder, play, and create their own response.

Loosening the reins to create a public forum in which students articulate their learning can be scary, though. What if they haven't really learned anything? What if there is nothing to show? What if the foundation of trust and knowledge is not strong enough? What if they are not prepared? Sometimes students really are not ready. I had promised my students that I would not let them embarrass themselves. I would never put them in a situation that I thought they couldn't handle successfully. A coach would never ask an athlete to run the mile without training, preparing, and practicing for weeks before a meet. Nor should a teacher expect students to present work in public without comparable training, preparation, and rehearsal.

It can be difficult, however, to know when a group is ready. Sometimes a leap of faith is necessary—an educated leap, that is. Each time I considered whether or not to commit ourselves to doing the play, I fell back on the excuse that "these kids just aren't ready." I finally realized that if I wanted my students to be willing to experiment and take risks, then I had to model that behavior for them. If I wanted them to trust each other, I had to trust them and believe in them first. If I wanted them to see their own strengths and power, I had to stop focusing so exclusively on what they couldn't do and begin to recognize, encourage, and celebrate what they could do. Teaching can be like parenting. Our most powerful lessons are not so much in what we say as in what we do. We try to give our own children a foundation of values, boundaries, and caring, and then, at a certain point, we must let go and allow them to experiment with those tools.

Challenging the Culture of Correctness

What had kept me from doing these things? What makes it difficult for teachers and students to take risks? A major factor in most people's resistance to trying new things is fear of failure. We are all afraid of failure. The stakes can be high if we fail: ridicule from peers, disapproval from colleagues, reprimands from bosses or teachers, one's own loss of self-esteem.

Rather than being institutions that encourage risk-taking, learning from mistakes, and experimentation, schools have played a major role in inculcating that constant fear of failure. In some schools, students are actually punished for giving wrong answers. In many schools, there is clearly a right way and a wrong way to do things. Even in schools that want to encourage inquiry and creative thinking, the culture of correctness can be difficult to overcome.

One year, I had the opportunity to take a class with Eleanor Duckworth at the Harvard Graduate School of Education. In the first session, she invited her students to explore the many ways that people learn. We were given small baggies filled with four different kinds of beans. She asked us to see how many different combinations we could find: kidney, black, pinto, pea; black, pinto, pea, kidney; and so on. "Pay attention to the strategies you are using to figure this out," she said. "Is this a trick?" someone asked suspiciously. "I know there is a formula for this," someone else moaned. "I just can't remember what it is." The tension in the room grew as we all worried about getting the "right" answer and doing it the "right" way. After all, we were graduate students. We *should* know how to do this. What if we failed our first assignment? Although I clearly fell victim to the prevailing sense of distress in the room, I wondered: Where did this panic come from? Did it start in first grade when you raised your hand to answer a question and were humiliated by a teacher or peers for a "wrong" response? I wrote in my journal:

> The bean activity was hard. I had to fight against feeling stupid a lot. I knew there was a formula, but I didn't know what it was. . . . It was such a struggle to pay attention to the process and not the answer. All those layers of feelings—self-doubt, stupidity, feeling slow, getting it right—are such distractions from the learning process. It made me think about kids and the culture we create in schools. . . . Even when Eleanor kept encouraging us to play, observe, examine and to not worry about [getting the right answer], we are so conditioned that judgment and right or wrong are always lurking around the corner. I see it in my students. They don't trust adults when we say, "Say what you think. We aren't making judgments." Because they know that deep down inside, we are.

There is certainly no doubt that there are right and wrong answers at times. One plus one makes two, not three or five or zero. But we also know that there can be more than one way to solve a problem. We know that critical thinking skills are developed as we explore and analyze options, not memorize a correct answer. If we focus so much on "right" answers, are we inadvertently creating a climate that closes rather than opens minds? In looking at students' work, do we see what is strong and not just what is wrong? Do we use language that silences children rather than gives them permission to try without fearing failure? Are we paying attention to the culture in each of our classrooms as to whether all students have a voice and can feel free to offer an idea, even if it doesn't work?

A respected colleague of mine, a math teacher, started thinking about this question. Steve Barkin's classroom is far from chaotic, but it is lively. Students are often engaged in spirited dialogue about math. Steve observed, however, that certain students tended to dominate these discussions. He noticed that when more confident and aggressive stu-

dents called out answers (right or wrong ones!), other students gradually receded, became more passive in class, and stopped participating.
When he asked the quiet ones what was going on, they described fear—
fear of failure and fear of ridicule, not from him, but from their peers.

Steve recognized that, in order to engage these students in learning
math, he had to create a culture of safety in the class. He established
strict rules about not calling out and shared his reasons with the class.
He explained that everyone needed to feel comfortable answering a
question or trying to solve a problem. Giving a wrong answer was far
preferable to not giving any answer. In fact, wrong answers can be quite
useful. They can help a teacher know where a student needs more
instruction or support. They can sometimes lead to great new ideas. With
the institution of the new rules, Steve started seeing more and more
students engage in class discussion. And, yes, their test scores went up.

Setting the Bar High

In challenging the "culture of correctness," we are not settling for
mediocrity in children's work. On the contrary, by freeing students and
ourselves from the fear of failure, we are able to expect far more of them.
How can schools encourage risk-taking and experimentation, allow
children to make mistakes without feeling stupid or humiliated, and
yet, at the same time, maintain high expectations and standards? First,
it is critical to set the bar high. Most students are capable of far better
work than what is asked of them. In fact, students are quite astute at
figuring out just how much a teacher expects of them and, therefore,
just how much they need to exert themselves. Students have described
this practice to me in great detail. Interestingly enough, it is usually
the teachers whose expectations are highest whom young people respect
the most. After all, students are getting the message from these teachers
that they are intelligent and capable of excellence.

Students know the difference between quality and shabby work.
Although critique protocols should first acknowledge strengths in the
work being reviewed, praising mediocrity should never be condoned.
Students (and teachers) have asked me, "But what if there is nothing
good to say?" Ninety-nine times out of 100, if we look closely before jump-
ing to judgment, we will find some strength in the work. An essay might
have an intriguing thesis. A story might have something as small as

one colorful phrase. But the recognition must be for something real. The rare times I have found nothing positive to say, it was because the student had not made a sincere effort to do the work. When Markie and her group first presented me with their rather silly scene on slavery, for example, I had to be honest with them. I could acknowledge the difficulty of their task, but I had to draw my line in the sand about what I expected of them. What they first presented to me was not acceptable. They needed to think about their goals and try again.

Trying Again

"Try again" is the key to building toward excellence. Certainly professional writers, artists, architects, planners don't expect to "get it just right" on the first draft. If our goal is high-quality work and real learning, we need to give children the opportunity to go "back to the drawing board" without feeling put down. Have we taught students both the value and habit of critique and revision? When students get something wrong or don't do the best job that they could, do they have the opportunity to try again? Are they asked to rewrite a paper that is poorly organized, or do they just receive a poor grade? A year after our play, some of my students visited me with reports from high school. Regine said, "When you get your papers back now, the teachers just put a grade on it and they don't tell you why. When I asked why, they said that is the grade they feel you deserve. They didn't explain it." Tessa added, "They don't do critique groups there. You just pass in your paper and get graded on it. I think our critique groups really helped in people's work . . . we realized that what we write has to be presentable to other people."

Do students have the opportunity to evaluate their own successes and failures? Do we ask them to think about their own learning and to take ownership of it? Ron Berger (1997) emphasizes that the most important assessment in schools is done by students, not teachers.

> Every student carries around with him or her a picture of acceptable standards, a notion of what his or her work should look like before it is handed in or before it is a finished piece. This picture is a vision of how accurate, neat, thorough, original, and elegant a piece of work should be. This should be a vital concern of every school: What is the picture of quality in the

heads of our students? Not our "gifted" students or our "motivated" students, but what is it in *all* our students? . . . And, most important, how can we get into the heads of our students and sharpen that picture as needed? (p. 29)

After all, if we are pursuing high standards, we want our students to have internalized them by the time they leave us.

A number of years ago, Steve, our math teacher, started asking students to analyze their mistakes on a test. He gave them three categories. "Is this a 'dumb' mistake, like you added two plus two and got five? Did you solve a different problem? Or have you not really mastered the concept? You just don't get how to divide fractions yet." With each test analysis, students were able to articulate what they needed to be more successful next time. Some saw patterns in their errors. One student said, "I kept making lots of dumb mistakes. I realized I was hurting my own grade just because I never took the time to go over my answers before I turned in my paper."

Not all students love the chance to revisit their work. When you push students to do their best, some of them will kick and scream and resist and fight you at first, as my class did when we started the Expert Project books. They will give you all the reasons why they can't do the work, why they've done the best they can, why you are expecting too much of them. It is easy to begin to doubt yourself, but it is critical to resist that doubt. This is the hard work of growth and learning. As Frederick Douglass said, "Without struggle, there is no progress."

But doubt and weariness can creep in. What if I am expecting more than this child can do? I have wondered. What if I am pushing too hard? Am I setting this child up for failure? Do I want to read this set of papers yet one more time? Maybe we should just settle for what was done and move on. Students, especially those who feel little ownership or investment in their work yet, will urge you to let them off the hook. I have seen many teachers capitulate to poor-quality work at this point.

Providing Clear Criteria and Feedback

This is where clear criteria come in. Many students have complained to me that they hate redrafting their work. When I push them about why, one common response is that they don't really understand *why* they are revising it. For many students, revising means copying a paper over again with spelling and punctuation corrections. It is not enough to tell students to go back and "do it again." They must be able to see *how* they can make the work better. Feedback needs to be clear and concrete. "You need to add supporting detail to this paragraph." "You can make the lettering much neater if you use a ruler or a light table." "If you slow down and emphasize the consonant sounds, your speech will be clearer." "You solved the first part of the problem but not the second. Try again."

In fact, by developing clear criteria and a working language of critique with students before entering a project or assignment, you are providing a road map for them to guide their work. This can be painstaking and difficult at times. When I first started doing this, I felt I was just slowing everything down. But gradually, I saw students take more ownership of the criteria and really internalize them. If we insist on the process of critique and revision while providing students with the "language of critique," students amaze themselves with the quality of their own work.

Taking the Time

All this takes time, and time is a tight commodity in most schools. Especially when there is a lot of external pressure to "cover the curriculum," it can be difficult to allow the time to draft and redraft work, to analyze mistakes, or to rehearse and critique a speech before presenting it to the class. Those faced with teaching 500 years of history in one year or covering 40 chapters in a science book know this pressure only too well.

During my visit with play graduates Regine and Tessa, I asked them about their history classes in high school. Regine responded, "The history that *we* did with you was the best history I ever did because we worked together. Now they just give you textbooks, ask you to write from the textbook, answer questions, take the test. In history class here, you got to work with people. If you didn't know the answer, other people would teach you. You communicated with others. It's not like a textbook kind of thing."

"Yeah," Tessa added, "we had more time. In high school, we have to cover like five chapters a week. I don't really learn anything. You copy stuff out of the book. You don't get it in your head."

How can we develop real "habits of mind" if we are so focused on covering, rather than *un*covering, the curriculum? Deborah Meier (1995) argues,

> There is no way to spend the time needed on strong intellectual habits if one is whizzing through academic terrain at the speed required to cover it, and no way to engage all young people when the choice of subject matter isn't rooted in real inquiry on the part of teachers and students alike. (p. 172)

In the rush to get through a unit and on to the next, teachers can be more concerned about where the class is supposed to be than where our students actually are. Have we "covered" a lesson without giving students time to really practice the skill or to experiment with the concept? If, through some form of assessment (a test, a project, a class discussion), we realize that a class does not understand what we think we taught, are we ready to stop, review, reteach, examine closely what hasn't worked? Or if something has broken down in the community, as happened on our trip to Mt. Monadnock, are we willing to put aside the daily lesson plan to address the problem?

Making Choices: Less Is More

This does not mean that schools shouldn't maintain high standards, rigorous expectations, and clear accountability about what is taught. It does mean that we need to recognize that we can't do it all if we want to do it well, and thus we must make certain choices. School communities need to have thoughtful and informed conversations about what is essential for students to know and be able to do. Several years ago, Ted Sizer (1989), founder of the Coalition of Essential Schools, wrote:

> The school's goals should be simple: that each student master a limited number of essential skills and areas of knowledge. While these skills and areas will, to varying degrees, reflect the traditional academic disciplines, the program's design should be shaped by the intellectual and imaginative powers and competencies that students need, rather than by "subjects" as conventionally defined. . . . Curricular decisions should be guided by the aim of thorough student mastery and achievement rather than by an effort merely to "cover content." (p. 2)

One of the 10 principles of the Coalition of Essential Schools, the aphorism "less is more" invites teachers to cover fewer subjects in greater depth. This allows teachers to focus on real understanding and achievement. It allows students time to own their learning. In social studies, this means not trying to cover 200 years of American history in 1 year. It may mean having to choose between going into depth on the industrial revolution or the Civil War. But by delving deeply into the social, political, and economic threads that weave the cloth of that era, students gain a profound understanding of how history is made. In literature, it may mean performing *Romeo and Juliet* rather than just reading it. When students become a character, they begin to understand the language, motivation, and actions with much more insight. In writing, students ideally wouldn't write a new piece each week but rather two or three polished stories or essays over a term, so as to give the writers time for critique that would guide them in making deep, thoughtful revisions. It is through feedback and the opportunity to re-view their own work that students really grow as writers.

Engaging in Meaningful Work

In addition to creating a climate of respect and mutual appreciation in the class, setting the bar high, and giving students time to explore curriculum more deeply, we must provide students with work that itself is meaningful. All learners engage most fully in a task when they see its purpose and find some relevance to their own lives. For many students, it is essential that they see some meaning or value to the work. "What's the point?" students often ask. "What has this got to do with me?" If the answer is "nothing," then we can easily lose that child. Or if the answer is "to get ready for high school," a few students will dutifully comply, but many will just check out. If we want our students to be critical thinkers and lifelong learners, then, as Deborah Meier (1995) says, "what our students think about our enterprise, whether it makes sense to them, is at the heart of the matter. If their schooling chiefly depends on their industry, then we must engage their industry" (p. 163). Students need to see some relevance between their lives and the overarching goals of a curriculum.

This does not mean that we study sex, drugs, and rock and roll. It does mean, however, that we engage in curriculum content with an eye toward relevancy and connections. The issues we explore must be authentic. When students see themselves in their work, they are much more likely to learn rather than just to memorize. For example, if students can connect the Chinese Exclusion Acts to their own experiences of exclusion (which we all have had), they understand that history in a deeper, more profound way. When we wonder aloud how the roots of slavery in our country have any connection to our cafeteria with tables of Black students on one side and White students on the other, students begin to listen. When we use statistical analysis to reveal patterns of gender discrimination, we understand our own relationships differently. Students need to see how increasing their knowledge gives them tools for better understanding themselves and the world around them.

True ownership of that knowledge comes when students are given the opportunity to give voice to their own learning. This can happen through the writing and production of a play, or the making of an original picture book. It can happen when math students design and build a model bridge or when students test the quality of water in their town (as Ron Berger's students did). It can happen when students are challenged to work through their own fears of and prejudices against people who are different from them, or engage in the democratic process about issues that impact their own lives. They must have an opportunity to make their own meaning of their learning and to put that meaning into practice.

What does it mean to be educated? Some people say it is knowing certain facts, certain information. There is no doubt that having key knowledge and information is critical to being literate in our society today. But being educated is not just knowing the facts. It is also knowing how to use information, how to analyze, synthesize, and transform what one has learned from others into something one knows for oneself. The foundation on which to build this deep engagement with curriculum has to be a climate of respect, trust, and mutual appreciation. Within the safety of that environment, students can focus on the scary but exciting process of creating and crafting original, high-quality work. Without that foundation, the work will rarely exceed mediocrity. This class had confirmed for me the fundamental connection between a positive, supportive democratic environment and high-quality work, academic achievement, and real understanding.

We were not able to luxuriate in our postproduction euphoria. A week later, our eighth graders graduated. They were heading on to a large urban high school with many new challenges. As I watched each one cross the stage to receive his or her diploma, I wondered how far they would carry the lessons from geese with them. Would they be secure enough in themselves to not need to put someone else down? Would they remember how they were capable of so much more than they first thought possible? Would they continue to hold themselves to high standards? Would they remember how powerful and creative they could be when they trusted and relied on each other?

Although we had undergone a powerful transformation as a class, I knew that there were no guarantees about individual growth. I had come to recognize over the year, both for myself and for my students, that the learning process is a slow and gradual one. All learners need multiple opportunities to practice and use new skills and knowledge in an authentic context. I knew that a seed had been planted. But just how far would it be able to grow? Without support, encouragement, and ongoing practice, these lessons from geese might fade. That is why I believe educators must engage in a thoughtful dialogue about the connections between what we teach and the culture in which we teach it, what we want our students to know and be able to do and *how* they use these tools of knowledge. We have to have a conversation about the kind of communities we want to live in and how we prepare our children to step into those communities as thoughtful citizens. We need to discuss not only the importance of academic achievement but also what we think real academic achievement is and toward what end do we pursue it.

Without that larger dialogue, the work is more difficult and less hopeful. We all know the power of one person to touch the life of a child. We know that seeds can be planted that blossom years later, sometimes in the most unexpected ways. Indeed, in the absence of other rewards or incentives, this belief fuels many of us to keep doing the hard work of teaching. But I can't help but wonder how many more lives could be touched, how much more our students would learn, and how less random our work would feel if we worked together to teach children to be human beings.

References

Beane, J. (1997). *Curriculum integration: Designing the core of democratic education*. New York: Teachers College Press.

Berger, R. (1997). *A culture of quality*. Providence, RI: Annenberg Institute for School Reform.

Coles, R. (1995, September 22). The disparity between intellect and character. *Chronicle of Higher Education*, p. A68.

Duckworth, E. (1996). *The having of wonderful ideas* (2nd ed.). New York: Teachers College Press.

Facing History and Ourselves National Foundation. (1994). *Facing history and ourselves: Holocaust and human behavior*. Brookline, MA: Author.

Fulghum, R. (1993). *All I really need to know I learned in kindergarten: Uncommon thoughts on common things*. New York: Fawcett.

Gardner, H. (1993). *Multiple intelligences: The theory in practice*. New York: Basic Books.

Glickman, C. (1993). *Renewing America's schools: A guide for school-based action*. San Francisco: Jossey-Bass.

Haley, A. (1976). *Roots*. New York: Doubleday.

Hawkins, D. (1980, Autumn). On getting involved in history. *Outlook, 37*, 24.

Korty, C. (1979). *On the line*. Available from the author at 1 Fitchburg St., Apt. C321, Somerville, MA 02143.

Lester, J. (1968). *To be a slave*. New York: Scholastic.

Lewis, C., Schaps, E., & Watson, M. (1996, September). The caring classroom's academic edge. *Educational Leadership*, pp. 16–21.

Lowry, L. (1993). *The giver*. Boston: Houghton Mifflin.

Meier, D. (1995). *The power of their ideas*. Boston: Beacon Press.

Morales, R. (1986). I am what I am. In A. Morales & R. Morales, *Getting home alive* (pp. 138–139). Ithaca, NY: Firebrand Books.

National Commission on Excellence in Education. (1983). *A nation at risk: The imperative for educational reform*. Washington, DC: U.S. Government Printing Office.

Noddings, N. (1999, April). Renewing democracy in schools. *Phi Delta Kappan*. p. 580.

Richter, R. (1953). *The light in the forest*. New York: Bantam.

Shirts, R. (1977). *Bafa bafa: A cross culture simulation*. Del Mar, CA: Simile II.

Sizer, T. (1989). *Diverse practice, shared ideas: The essential school*. Providence, RI: Coalition of Essential Schools.

Strom, M., & Parsons, W. (1982). *Facing history and ourselves: Holocaust and human behavior*. Watertown, MA: Intentional Educations.

Walters, J., Veenema, S., Pace, J., & Meyaard, J. (1990). *Immigrant 1850*. Cambridge, MA: Harvard University Graduate School of Education.

Wells, M. Cyrene. (1996). *Literacies lost: When students move from a progressive middle school to a traditional high school*. New York: Teachers College Press.

Index

Academic curriculum, xv
Adulthood, child's transition to, ix
Africans, 56, 63–65
*All I Really Need to Know I Learned
    in Kindergarten* (Fulghum),
    xiv
American Dream theme, 3

BAFA BAFA (game), 44–46, 71–72
Barkin, Steve, 117–118
Bay, John, 77
Beane, James, xvii
Berger, Ron, xviii, xix, 119–120
Bilingual students, 25–26
Blacks, 56, 63–66
Body sculpture, 74
Book Talk Groups, 2

Chanting activity, 78–80
Character traits, 13
Child Development Project, xvii–xviii
Chinese immigrants, 58, 61
Choice system, 2, 122–123
City Sites project, 65–66
Civil rights movement theme, 3–4, 56
Classroom community. *See also*
    Community theme; Culture of
    the classroom
    enhancing academic learning
        through, xiv–xv
    importance of, ix, xvii
    summer camp compared with
        school, 5–6

Class size, 2
Coalition of Essential Schools, 3,
    122–123
Community theme, 6–7. *See also*
    Theater in the classroom
    "community" tests, 9–11, 12
    defining community, 9–12, 113–
        114
    field trip for ice skating, 50–52
    field trip to Mt. Monadnock, 18–21
    goal setting, 12–15
    literature studies, 41–46
    parable of the geese, 17–18, 21
    sameness and difference, 39–46
    simulation of cultural differences,
        44–46
    teacher learning in, 114–125
    theater in the classroom and, 16–
        17
Critical thinking skills, 117
Cultural differences
    exclusion and, 58–61, 71
    immigrant populations and,
        53–61
    literature studies and, 41–44, 47–
        50, 63
    poetry and, 54–55
    simulation of, 44–46
Culture of classroom. *See also*
    Classroom community
    challenging culture of correctness,
        116–118
    quality of school and, xix

Culture of classroom (*continued*)
  theater theme and, 4–5. *See also*
    Theater in the classroom
  time spent developing community
    in, xiv, 121–122
Curriculum
  academic, xv
  Facing History and Ourselves, 3,
    99–100
  integrated, thematic approach to,
    xv, 2
  rich, deep, xvii
  social, xv

Daily Edit, 2
Democratic community
  as apprenticeship in liberty, xv
  in classroom, ix
  power of, xviii–xix
Dewey, John, xv
Discrimination. *See also* Cultural
    differences
  immigrant population and, 53–61
  impact of, xiv–xv
Douglass, Frederick, 120
Drama. *See* Theater in the
    classroom
Duckworth, Eleanor, 115, 116–118

Emerson, Ralph Waldo, xvi
Escalante, Jaime, xviii
"Essential" questions, 3
Exclusion, 58–61, 71
  stories of, 58–60
  visual image of, 60–61
Expert Projects, 22–38
  difficulties of, 34–35
  Expertise Project Proposal, 25–26
  introduction, 23–24
  peer critique and revision, 26–31
  phases of, 24–25, 35–38
  standards for excellence, 26, 31–34
Eye of the Storm (film), xiv–xv

Facing History and Ourselves
  curriculum, 3, 99–100

Feedback, 27–30, 120–121
Field trips
  ice skating, 50–52
  to Mt. Monadnock, 18–21
Flocking activity, 77–78
Frontline episode, 65
Fulghum, R., xiv

Games
  simulation, 44–46, 71–72
  theater, 77–80
Gardner, Howard, 13
Giver, The (Lowry), 41–43
Glickman, Carl, xv
Goal setting, 12–15
Graham and Park School
    (Cambridge, Mass.)
  described, 1–3
  humanities classes, 2–5, 6–7
  summer camp compared with, 5–6

Haley, Alex, 63
Having of Wonderful Ideas, The
    (Duckworth), 115
Hawkins, David, 58
Hendricks, Newell, 98–103
Holocaust theme, xvi, 3

"I Am What I Am" (Morales), 54–55, 71
Ice skating trip, 50–51
Immigrant 1850 (simulation
    program), 55–56
Immigration. *See also* Cultural
    differences
  African, 63–65
  Chinese, 58, 61
  computer simulation, 55–56
  exclusion and, 58–61
  Irish, 55–56, 58
Interdependencies, 65–66
Irish immigrants, 55–56, 58

Korty, C., 4, 93

Lester, Julius, 63
Lewis, C., xviii

Light in the Forest, The (Richter), 43–44, 47–50, 68, 72
Literacies Lost (Wells), xviii
Literature studies
　The Giver (Lowry), 41–43
　The Light in the Forest (Richter), 43–44, 47–50, 68, 72
Lowry, Lois, 41

Meaningful work, 123–125
Meier, Deborah, ix–x, xvii, 122, 123
Meyaard, J., 55
Miniprofiles of students, 13–14, 23–24
Morales, Rosario, 54
Multigrade classrooms, 2
Multiple intelligences (Gardner), 13
Music development, 98–103

National Commission on Excellence in Education, xvi
Nation at Risk, A, xvi
Nazi Germany, xvi, 3
Noddings, N., xv

On the Line (Korty), 4–5, 93–94
Ownership, 15, 30, 124

Pace, J., 55
Parable of the geese, 17–18, 21
Parsons, W., xvi, 3
Peer critique, 26–31, 118–119
　fear of, 28
　modeling, 28–30
　positive and specific feedback in, 27–30, 120–121
　usefulness of, 28
Plays. *See* Theater in the classroom
Poetry, 54–55
Project Zero, 55–56

Race and racism, 64–65
Real-world experiences, City Sites project, 65–66
Research. *See* Expert Projects
Richter, Conrad, 43–44

Risk-taking, 115–116
Roots (Haley), 63

Schaps, E., xviii
Shirts, R., 44
Simulation games, BAFA BAFA, 44–46, 71–72
Sizer, Ted, 122
Social curriculum, xv
Standardized test scores, 2
Standards for excellence
　Expert Projects, 26, 31–34
　theater in the classroom, 74–75, 118–119
Stories, x
　of exclusion, 58–60
Strom, M., xvi, 3
Studebaker Theater Company, 77
Student council, respect and, 39, 50

Teacher learning, 114–125
Theater in the classroom
　adding music to, 98–103
　based on *The Light in the Forest* (Richter), 47–50
　beginning work on, 67–75
　developing interest in, 62
　discussion of outcomes, 69–72
　final performance, 110–112
　finding the story, 82–87
　first week of working on play, 80–81
　lack of interest in, 16–17
　On the Line (play), 4–5, 93–94
　opening night, 105–110
　outline of play, 83, 84
　performances, 104–112
　scene development, 84–97
　standards for excellence, 74–75, 118–119
　teacher learning in, 114–125
　theater games and activities, 77–80
　tool box for developing, 68–69
　warm-up routine, 76–77, 83, 84

Themes of humanities class, 3–5, 6–7

To Be a Slave (Lester), 63, 68

Tocqueville, Alexis de, xv

"True Colors" video (*Front Line*), 65, 70–71

Trying again, 119–120

Veenema, S., 55

Vocabulary development, 2–3

Walters, J., 55

Warm-up routine, 76–77, 83, 84

Watson, M., xviii

Wells, M. Cyrene, xviii

About the Author

Kathy Greeley received her B.A. in history at Oberlin College in 1975 and started teaching in 1980 after receiving an M.Ed. from Tufts University. She has been teaching at the Graham and Parks School in Cambridge, Massachusetts, as a seventh- and eighth-grade humanities teacher since 1989. In 1995, she took a year off from the classroom to attend the Harvard Graduate School of Education as a Conant Fellow. She has worked as a consultant to Expeditionary Learning/Outward Bound, a New America Schools project, and has worked closely with Project Zero at Harvard University and Facing History and Ourselves in Brookline, Massachusetts. She has published articles about teaching in *Freedom's Plough: Teaching in the Multicultural Classroom* (Routledge), *Social Issues, Service Learning and Community Service at the Middle Level* (Allyn and Bacon), and the *Harvard Educational Review*. She currently lives in Cambridge with her husband and two teenage daughters.